FRANCIS POULENC

Francis Poulenc: a recent portrait

FRANCIS POULENC

by

HENRI HELL

Translated from the French and introduced by
EDWARD LOCKSPEISER

GROVE PRESS, INC.
NEW YORK

Grove Press Books and Evergreen Books

are published by Barney Rosset at Grove Press, Inc.

64 University Place   New York 3, N.Y.

MANUFACTURED IN GREAT BRITAIN

CONTENTS

	Page
PREFACE	ix

I

La *Rapsodie Nègre* to *Les Biches*   1
(1899–1924)

II

Cinq Poèmes de Ronsard to the Organ Concerto   31
(1925–1938)

III

The Sextet to *La Fraîcheur et le Feu*   59
(1939–1950)

IV

The *Stabat Mater* to the Flute Sonata   77
(1951–1958)

V

Poulenc's Style. A Portrait   87

CATALOGUE AND INDEX OF WORKS   93

DISCOGRAPHY   107

INDEX   116

ILLUSTRATIONS

Francis Poulenc: a recent portrait   *Frontispiece*

opposite page

Poulenc's home at Noizay   8

Eluard and Apollinaire by Picasso   9

'Les Six' by Cocteau   24

Poulenc and Auric by Cocteau   25

Manuscript of music for *Jacques Villon*   40

Peter Pears in *Les Mamelles de Tirésias*   41

Stage set by Osbert Lancaster for *Les Mamelles de Tirésias*   56

Nikitina and Lifar in *Les Biches*   57

Jean Cocteau and 'Les Six'   72

Laurencin and Apollinaire by Henri Rousseau   73

Francis Poulenc today   88

PREFACE

In the golden decline of our musical civilisation, Francis Poulenc is one of the most endearing survivals. Paradox, conundrums and spoof are his natural attributes. But this is only the superficial side of this Fernandel among composers. This intelligent French musician is also a child-like primitive, the last of the lyrical composers, a remote offspring of Franz Schubert.

One immediately catches sight of Francis Poulenc, 'a big, countrified fellow, bony and jovial', as he appears in the sketch by Colette, hair *en brosse*, looking like an overgrown schoolboy and sending everyone around into fits of laughter. He has been telling one of his racy tales, heavily spiced with his native argot and sailing perilously near the wind. But the raconteur can also be an innocent who will listen quietly to what you say with an almost spaniel-like expression of wonder and sadness on his big, doggy face. Look also at the hands—great, bony structures that, at the keyboard, can stretch over an octave and a half. One doesn't have hands like that for nothing.

On the face of it, what kind of sinister mating is suggested by this cross-breeding of the pawky humour of a comedian and the lyrical sweetness of a musical genius? On the Fernandel side the line is clear enough—Fernandel, Maurice Chevalier, Louis Beydts, Messager—we are here approaching slightly more respectable spheres—and ultimately Emmanuel Chabrier.

Ever since the vivacious Chabrier burst on to the musical scene ('He is my true grandfather', acknowledges Poulenc), some kind of deliberate vulgarity crept into music and was conscientiously cultivated in an ironic spirit of defiance. It looks as if the treatment of overblown music-hall tunes in Chabrier was a musical equivalent of what Verlaine called *la nostalgie de la boue*. Like those flowers of melody of Poulenc himself, the engaging music of Chabrier is the easiest to fall for; and it is the easiest to be misunderstood. For this adorable, chubby-faced composer, the friend of Verlaine, Manet and Renoir, the worshipper of Wagner too, was the first of the inscrutable race of musical ironists—inscrutable because their very nature is a mask. Sincerity is no virtue in their eyes. But agility, a faithless agility of the heart, is.

The man is his music. The double strain of innocence and extravagant humour in Poulenc has well-known origins in French music. It reaches back, as I have suggested, to Chabrier, but more recently to Erik Satie, *bon oncle* of the band of composers proclaimed as *Les Six*. This 'sweet medieval musician who had strayed into our century by mistake', as he was described by his most eminent admirer, was also something of an Alice-in-Wonderland composer. Anxious that his appearances in the Paris musical world should not go unnoticed, he would appear on a concert platform in a fireman's shining brass helmet.

And so it came about that these butterflies, these children of music, were condemned to a tireless search for an identification that would fit. Who were they, what were they? None could ever fit. And they thus resigned themselves to making a note of beauty where it was to be found and sadly, infinitely sadly, making a joke of it. Paradoxically speaking, was this not a more touching form of sincerity than any other? I am sure that the race of these Chabriers, Saties and Poulencs, so simple at heart, so sensitive to sham, saw their vocation as Anatole France, in *The Garden of Epicurus*, saw his, inspired by an irony that was 'gentle and kindly disposed, mocking neither love nor beauty, disarming anger, teaching us to laugh at rogues and fools whom we might otherwise be so weak as to hate'.

Nowadays all music prides itself on being derivative. Stravinsky derives from Bach, Schoenberg from Mozart. The common pastime, among connoisseurs of modern music, is to spot resemblances. Our desperate eclecticism has almost obliterated our cherished notions of style. We struggle, though we may not always succeed, to make Voltaire's optimistic prophecy, *Tous les genres sont bons hormis le genre ennuyeux*, come true.

When, however, very rarely, the model is lyrical melody of the diatonic composers, this is quaintly considered altogether beyond the pale. The reason for this is that diatonic melody, the most beautiful of all musical gifts, is also the most inimitable. It was, moreover, possessed by only a few of the Romantic composers: besides Schubert, they were Chopin, Schumann, Tchaikovsky, Strauss, and I should add Prokofiev. These are precisely the composers who have nurtured the outstanding lyrical gifts of Poulenc. No composer of our time has so consistently worked in the purest forms of diatonic harmony—a means of expression long considered outworn (as indeed Stravinsky has considered all

other forms of harmony), though Poulenc has shown that
the special magic of diatonic harmony, modulation, un-
cluttered by wrong notes, can sometimes, even today, make
an effect as poignant as in Schubert himself.

Sweetness, however, can pall, as today may even a
genuine lyrical gift. Occasionally, therefore, some kind
of terrifying spectre is made to burst through Poulenc's
lyrical façade. 'There sometimes enters into his music',
André Schaeffner observes, 'a devil, some kind of
unruly child or a creature possessed who, in a flash,
turns everything into confusion, jumbles one style with
another, stops at no extravagance, pushes in a street song
or music-hall hit, keys up his harmony and rhythm to the
sophisticated standards of polytonality, the resultant chaos
including, too, a bit of jazz or imitation Blues. Exposed,
then, are those features, which he has no intention of hiding,
of raucousness, crowing and swagger.' And Schaeffner
concludes: 'The best and the worst of Poulenc collide in
these outbursts, though in time such irrational elements may
be seen to be at the core of the composer's inspiration.'[1]

At first sight, it would seem that Poulenc's allegiance to
nineteenth-century harmony would completely remove his
art from the contemporary scene and suggest some kind of
offshoot of Tchaikovsky and Massenet. In a sense this is
true. I do not think there is any doubt that the element most
admired by Poulenc in the work of Debussy, for instance,
is just the unmistakable strain in this composer of Massenet.
The introspective aspects of such works of Debussy as the
Nocturnes and the *Images* hardly touch his much more

[1] *Contrepoints* (Paris, January, 1946).

concrete world. Nor has he the slightest sympathy with
the similarly inturned mind of Fauré ('I cannot bear to
listen to his Requiem; it is one of the few things in music I
really detest.'). The exuberant Richard Strauss, on the other
hand, is a composer after Francis Poulenc's heart.

*   *   *

The bulk of Poulenc's work consists of well over a
hundred songs, nearly all of them neatly filling the framework of the perfect vignette. Not since Fauré has such a
corpus of original and beautiful songs been added to
French music, or indeed to the song literature of any country. The standard is uniformly high: they are remarkable
for a sensitive approach to the problems of musical prosody,
a lyrical exuberance and a warmth of feeling for the
human voice that has become extremely rare.

Poulenc learnt the art of song-writing, we learn from
M. Hell's study, from accompanying his distinguished
interpreter, Pierre Bernac, in the Lieder. I do not think,
however, that the appeal of Poulenc's songs is likely to
be enhanced by a purely musical analysis: simplicity itself
marks the generous flow of the melodic line and the easy
harmonic sequences. The charm and sophistication of
Poulenc's songs derive from their poetic inspiration. Here,
the composer has consciously identified himself with the
work of three poets, Max Jacob, Guillaume Apollinaire
and Paul Eluard, little known in England and worth dwelling
on to see the cast of his literary and musical mind.

Max Jacob (1876-1944) was a sardonic poet, whose inspiration was the burlesque. Gide likened him to Heine. Originally
B

an Alsatian Jew, Jacob was a converted Catholic, made his
home for a time in Brittany, lived in Montmartre as a
vagabond Bohemian and, a born actor, persistently mystified
his friends by his unexpected guises. Was he a business man,
his friends wondered, a connoisseur (with his monocle), a
church beadle, or the Prefect of Police (whom he is said to have
resembled)? When he rolled his eyes, he is said to have had
the wild look of an El Greco. His comic symbolism was
fearless. In his view of the vegetable kingdom, an artichoke
is a pregnant woman, a turnip a ponderous, obstinate
argument:

> L'artichaut est bourgeois, discret
> Ainsi qu'une mondaine enceinte
> Les tomates ont des regrets
> Et les poireaux des pudeurs saintes
> Le radis rose est un abbé de cour
> Le navet est opiniâtre et lourd.

Puns came to Max Jacob more naturally than rhymes,
even under the most tragic circumstances. The Gestapo, who
imprisoned him during the war, was the *J'ai ta peau*. He
tortured himself with parody, but Poulenc's settings of his
poems emphasise, in *Le Bal Masqué*, a less rasping view of his
humour and, in the *Cinq Poèmes*, a remote child-like sweetness:

> 'Si mon marin vous le chassez
> Au cimetière, vous me mettez
> Rose blanche, rose blanche et rose rouge.'

A poet of wider scope with whom Poulenc has been associated ever since his early cycle, *Le Bestiaire*, is Guillaume Apollinaire. This adopted name was a Gallicised abbreviation of Wilhelm-Apollinaris de Kostrowitski. The illegitimate son of a Polish noblewoman—it had been rumoured that his father had been the Pope—he was the discoverer, about 1912, of the Douanier Rousseau and the prominent leader of Bohemian life in Montparnasse. In his early days he had been unjustly imprisoned for having stolen the Mona Lisa from the Louvre, with the result that the bewildered poet begot an Apollinaire legend. His English biographer, Roger Shattuck, surveys his activities under the headings of 'a clown, a scholar, a drunkard, a gourmet, a lover, a criminal, a devout Catholic, a wandering Jew, a soldier and a good husband'.[1]

In his theatrical farce, *Les Mamelles de Tirésias*, used by Poulenc as the libretto for his comic opera, Apollinaire unites the worlds of surrealism and the music-hall. In his introduction to this fantasy on the change of sexes which, incidentally, he wrote for an intensely serious purpose— Apollinaire believed that the French were neglecting the act of love—he has this to say on the origin of the Surrealist movement: 'When man wanted to imitate walking, he invented the wheel which has no connection whatever with a leg. This was an unconscious surrealist example.'

Apollinaire's amorous poetry is simple and intense (notably in the collection *Ombre de mon amour*), his

1 *Selected writings of Guillaume Apollinaire*. Translated with a critical introduction by Roger Shattuck (London, 1950). Another illuminating English study on Apollinaire has been published by C. M. Bowra (Horizon, London, 1945).

demand for identification imperative, his cynical despon-
dency courageous and also pitiless. Roger Shattuck makes
the point that in *Le Bestiaire* 'every animal is somehow
received into his life to make its contribution—the camel to
allow him to travel, the crab to reveal to him his own
backwardness, the mouse to make him feel the gnawings of
despair'. The symbolism is wonderfully ingenious. And
significantly, it was a setting of this last desperate poem,
La Souris, that Poulenc, years after he had written the early
Apollinaire song-cycle, dedicated to Marya Freund, the
renowned interpreter of Schoenberg's *Pierrot Lunaire*.

Usually the more satirical of Apollinaire's poems have
been chosen by Poulenc. But he also underlines Apollinaire's
lyrical qualities, and very subtly this is done in the settings
of some of the poet's Parisian caricatures, notably in the
one called *Montparnasse* (from the collection *Il y a*):

O porte de l'hôtel avec deux plantes vertes
Vertes que jamais
Où sont mes fruits. Où me planté-je
O porte de l'hôtel un ange est devant toi
On n'a jamais si bien défendu la vertu
Distribuant des prospectus
Donnez-moi pour toujours une chambre à la semaine
Ange barbu vous êtes en réalité
Un poète lyrique d'Allemagne
Qui voulez connaître Paris
Vous connaissez de son pavé
Ces raies sur lesquelles il ne faut pas que l'on marche
Et vous rêvez

D'aller passer votre dimanche à Garches.

Il fait un peu lourd et vos cheveux sont longs
O bon petit poète un peu bête et trop blond
Vos yeux ressemblent tant à ces deux grands ballons
Qui s'en vont dans l'air pur
A l'aventure.[1]

The poetic world of Paul Eluard (1895-1952) has been the most profitable source of Poulenc's lyrical inspiration. Eluard's central theme is the diffusion and unselfishness of love: *T'aimer me rend à tous les hommes*. Maurois saw in this humanitarian something of Shelley. There is neither sensation nor sensuousness in his amorous poetry; nor is

---

1   O hotel door with two green plants
       Simply green
       Which never bear flowers
       Where are my fruits, where can I plant myself
       O door in front of you an angel stands
       Distributing prospectuses
       Never has virtue been so well protected
       Rent me a room at weekly rates for all time
       Bearded angel you are in reality
       A lyric German poet
       Who wishes to know Paris
       You know this pavement
       And the cracks on which one must not step
       And you dream
       Of spending Sunday at Garches.

       The air is heavy and your hair is long
       My little poet a little stupid and too blonde
       Your eyes look terribly like those two big balloons
       Which rise in the pure air
       To adventure.
                     Translation by Roger Shattuck

there intimacy; there is instead some sort of impersonal objectivisation of love, made universal and remote:

> 'Sous le ciel grand'ouvert la mer ferme ses ailes
> Aux flancs de ton sourire un chemin part de moi
> Rêveuse toute en chair lumière toute en feu
> Aggrave mon plaisir annule l'étendue
> Hâte-toi de dissoudre et mon rêve et ma vue.'[1]

In Poulenc's interpretations of these poets, the ironist and the lyricist are kept severely apart. In each sphere there are many variations and gradations, and these M. Hell has attempted to define. Guillaume Apollinaire and Max Jacob are the poets for banter (*le leg-Poulenc*, as a French critic has it); Paul Eluard for the numerous songs where—the *cliché* has here its real meaning—the composer simply writes with his heart. The choice is abundant in both categories. My own preference goes, in the first, to *Dans le jardin d'Anna*—a scream of a piece in Poulenc's best mock-sentimental style; and in the second to *Tu vois le feu du soir* and *Une herbe pauvre*, an affecting vision of a snowscape which has made me wonder whether Poulenc, in this Schubertian vein of his, might not one day go to the poetry of Rilke, and particularly to that religious poem, not unlike the Eluard text of this particular song, where Rilke, seized by the sight of the loveliest of wild flowers growing out of

[1]   Beneath wide sky the ocean folds its wings
       A road runs out of me to your smile's edge
       You dreamer all of flesh light all of flame
       Deepen my pleasure blot out distances
       Come quick dissolve my dreaming and my seeing.
                    Translation by Stephen Spender and Frances Cornford

stones between deserted railway tracks, suddenly under-
stands what is meant by the Poverty of God.

A large section of Poulenc's recent work, beginning with
the *Mass* of 1937, does in fact consist of a whole series of
religious choral works. The Black Virgin at the Sanctuary
of Rocamadour, and also a veneration for St Anthony of
Padua, are said by the composer to be the external origins
of his religious inspiration. Yet the simple fervour that
emanates from these intensely lyrical works has also
a more intimate and homely appeal. Sometimes, it is true,
the pure-of-heart composer who, even now, has no intention
of foresaking his *adorable mauvaise musique*, crosses the
religious boundary in the spirit of the juggler performing
his tricks before the Virgin at Notre-Dame. But more often,
in the *Litanies* and particularly the *Stabat Mater*, the most
expansive of these works, heard in England at the Three
Choirs Festival, a remarkable and telling simplicity comes
into Catholic religious music again. If pressed for an analogy,
I should look to the ingenuous Sainte Thérèse of Lisieux
perhaps, the 'Little Flower', playing with her ball. It is
music in which, as Jean Cocteau said of a distinguished
humorist who found salvation in the Church, 'L'esprit
chez lui rejoignit l'Esprit'.

In *The Carmelites*, the opera of devout Roman Catholic
inspiration illustrating the manifestation of Grace, and having
as its principal theme the wrestlings of an ingenuous soul
with fear, the heart of this master ironist has in the end
triumphed. One would not wish to underrate the size
of this musical and moral victory. At the least it
must enable us to review Poulenc's work in the spirit of the

heroine in Max Beerbohm's *Happy Hypocrite*, who finally sees her lover, the hypocrite, unmasked:

' "Surely," said Jenny, "your face is even dearer to me, even fairer than the semblance that hid it and deceived me . . . let me look always at your own face. Let the time of my probation be over. Kiss me with your own lips." So he took her in his arms, as though she had been a little child, and kissed her with his own lips. She put her arms round his neck, and he was happier than he had ever been. They were alone in the Garden now. Nor lay the mask any longer on the lawn, for the sun had melted it.'

It is in this frank, revealing spirit, that M. Henri Hell's book, presented here in an abridged form, will be a guide to both the gay and the grave aspects of Poulenc's affecting art.

1959   E.L.

I

(1 8 9 9 - 1 9 2 4)
La Rapsodie Nègre to *Les Biches*

FRANCIS POULENC, the son of Emile Poulenc and Jenny
Royer, was born in Paris on January 7th, 1899, at 2 Place
des Saussaies, not more than a few yards from the Presiden-
tial palace of the Elysée.

On his father's side his family were fervent Catholics
from Espalion in the department of Aveyron: a great-uncle
of the composer, the Abbé Joseph Poulenc, was the curé of
Ivry-sur-Seine. Poulenc's Catholic faith and the religious
inspiration of a large part of his work are closely bound to
these family roots.

His mother's family had for generations been of pure
Parisian stock descending from a long line of craftsmen—
cabinet-makers, tapestry-weavers and bronze-founders who
worked in the Faubourg St. Antoine. The Poulencs were
fond of music, but the Royers' interests covered a much
wider field; they kept abreast of the entire artistic world.
Thanks to 'Uncle Papoum', a keen amateur of the theatre,
who was a brother of the composer's mother, the young
Poulenc learnt about the great names of those days, Sarah
Bernhardt, Réjane, Lavallière and Lucien Guitry; and he
was more impressed by the pictures of these legendary
actors and actresses that used to appear in the *Théâtre illustré*
than by the old-fashioned illustrations in the books of the

I

Comtesse de Ségur forming part of the Bibliothèque Rose which lined the shelves of his home.

Music was the natural means of expression from his his childhood. Poulenc has spoken of his mother, who was a delightful amateur pianist, as having had faultless musical taste and a most lovely touch. As a boy, he was enraptured by her playing of Mozart, Chopin, Schubert and Schumann; and he was no less enraptured by pieces in a less lofty style which she used to play, notably a *Lullaby* by Grieg and a *Romance* by Anton Rubinstein. Even in those early years he had begun to be drawn to what he later called his *adorable mauvaise musique.*

At the age of five Francis began to learn the piano. At eight he started to work with Mlle Boutet de Monvel, a niece of César Franck and an excellent teacher, under whose guidance he used to practise regularly every evening after school. It was then, at the age of eight, that he first heard a work of Debussy, the *Danses sacrée et profane* for harp and string orchestra, by which he was immediately overcome: the attraction it had for him was in the suggestion of wrong notes. His one desire was to be able to find for himself the intriguing chords of the ninth in this work at the piano. Once awakened, this passion for Debussy was steadily to develop, though he was hardly able to play any of the piano works before the age of fourteen.

The winter of 1910 brought a revelation. Driven with his parents to Fontainebleau as a result of the floods which had turned Paris into a sort of Venice, he came across Schubert's *Winterreise* in a local music shop. He played over *Die Krähe, Der Lindenbaum, Der Leiermann* and particularly

the wonderful *Die Nebensonnen* again and again. There
was no stopping him. 'I turned the piano round,' he
wrote, 'so that at about four in the afternoon I could sing
the *Die Nebensonnen* whilst looking at the sun which
looked like a huge Dutch cheese moving through the rimy
trees of the forest.' Schubert's *Die Nebensonnen* was the song
that awakened his melodic gifts, to be illustrated nine years
later in *Le Bestiaire*.

Many discoveries were made in the meantime, the
most fruitful, after Debussy and Schubert, being the dis-
covery of Stravinsky's *Firebird* and *Petruchka* and, in 1914
when Poulenc was fifteen, of *Le Sacre du Printemps*, conducted
by Pierre Monteux at the Casino de Paris. The tremendous
impression made on him was looked at askance by his
father whose tastes went to Beethoven, Berlioz, César
Franck and Massenet, but not by his mother who was
inclined to let him go his own way.

In 1915 Poulenc made up his mind to concentrate on the
piano. He was at this time a great admirer of Ricardo
Viñès, the renowned interpreter of Fauré, Debussy and
Ravel, to whom he was introduced by a family friend,
Mme Geneviève Sienkiewicz. At his first lesson Poulenc
played Schumann's *Faschingschwank* and some Debussy
Preludes, among them *Minstrels*. Master and pupil immediately fell for each other. 'Viñès was a delightful
character,' the composer recalls, 'some kind of strange
Hidalgo with an enormous moustache, a brown sombrero
in true Barcelona style, and button boots with which he
used to kick me in the shins whenever I was clumsy at the
pedals. No one could teach the art of using the pedals, an

essential feature of modern piano music, better than Viñès. He somehow managed to extract clarity precisely from the ambiguities of the pedals. His *staccato* playing was equally remarkable. Marcelle Meyer, his most brilliant pupil, declared that he made even *Petruchka* seem easy.'

Poulenc's debt to Viñès is incalculable, in regard to both his own manner of playing and the originality of his keyboard writing. Moreover, it was through Viñès that Poulenc met two musicians who were to have a far-reaching effect on his work, Erik Satie and Georges Auric.

Satie was at first somewhat distrustful of 'the white-headed boy'. But any hesitation on his part was overcome by Poulenc's genuine enthusiasm for Satie's ballet *Parade*, produced by Diaghilev's Russian Ballet in 1917. The composer has confessed to an 'immediate and wide influence made by Satie on both the spiritual and musical planes'. Alfred Cortot has rightly said of the *Mouvements perpétuels* that these three pieces were 'reflections of the ironical outlook of Satie adapted to the sensitive standards of the current intellectual circles'. This admiration of Poulenc has remained, and he has still the authentic manner of conveying the curious appeal of Satie's piano pieces.

Georges Auric, who was of the same age, became a sort of spiritual or older brother, remarkable, in Poulenc's eyes, for his precocious gifts. Darius Milhaud recalls how Auric 'astounded me by his learning, intelligence and facility. The early manuscripts he used to show me were remarkable for a combination of youthful freshness, a high degree of skill and an appealing element of banter.' Poulenc has spoken of him in similar terms: 'Music by the precocious Auric was

heard at the *Société Nationale* when the composer was no
more than fourteen. At fifteen he used to discuss sociology
with Léon Bloy, and at seventeen, theology with Jacques
Maritain. Apollinaire asked the young Auric's advice on his
play *Les Mamelles de Tirésias*. I was immediately attracted
by his knowledge and we became the closest of friends.'
Today, forty years later, their friendship is on the same
footing. They shared a similar musical outlook and the
same admiration for Satie and Stravinsky. They were
together in the first performance of *Les Noces*, playing two
of the four piano parts, and Diaghilev produced their
ballets *Les Biches* and *Les Fâcheux* within a few days of each
other. Throughout the years Auric has consistently been his
contemporary's most trusted guide and mentor.

A prominent figure of those days to whom Viñès
introduced his pupil was the singer Jeanne Bathori, who had
introduced many of the songs of Fauré, Debussy, Ravel
and Satie, and through whom Poulenc met Arthur Honegger.
From this period, too, dates his friendship with Germaine
Tailleferre and Louis Durey. The close association with
Darius Milhaud dates from a tennis party at a slightly
earlier period. The younger composer had admiringly
asked for Milhaud's signature, only to be gently but firmly
rebuffed. They were, however, to come very closely
together on Milhaud's return in 1919 from Brazil, where he
had been in the diplomatic service as secretary to Paul
Claudel, and at the home of the poet René Chalupt.

Apart from these new musical friends, Poulenc was
greatly attracted to the young Raymonde Linassier, a friend
of his childhood days and now a girl of keen intelligence

and striking personality. Much was owed to Raymonde Linassier, 'La Violette noire', as Léon-Paul Fargue called her, throughout the composer's boyhood and adolescent years. Passionately fond of literature, she introduced Poulenc to the works of Claudel and Gide and later Proust and Joyce, and together they explored Verlaine, Mallarmé and especially Baudelaire. These early poetic experiences of Poulenc—he had known Mallarmé's *Apparition* by heart at the age of ten—were calculated to develop his remarkable sense of musical prosody. In the meantime Raymonde Linassier and Francis Poulenc were frequently to be seen together at Adrienne Monnier's bookshop *Aux Amis des Livres*, in the Rue de l'Odéon, the rendezvous of a literary élite that included Valéry, Gide, Claudel, Joyce, Valéry Larbaud, Apollinaire and Léon-Paul Fargue. Poulenc's friends in this literary circle were André Breton, Louis Aragon and Paul Eluard, whose poems were later to inspire him.

A barrister at the Paris Court of Appeal and also an archaeologist employed at the Musée Guimet, Raymonde Linassier died at an early age in 1932. Her quiet dignity and sensitive mind have been impressively portrayed by Léon-Paul Fargue and these are the memories cherished too by Poulenc who, years later, was to dedicate to her his ballet *Les Animaux modèles*.

★　　★　　★

Poulenc's first attempts at composition were pieces for the piano. They were preludes of incredible complexity

written out on three or four staves, later referred to by the
composer as inferior imitations of Debussy and Stravinsky.
One of them in which, as an adolescent, he took a particular
pride was bombastically entitled 'Processional for the
Cremation of a Mandarin', the opening of which was
modelled on the Chinese March from Stravinsky's *Nightin-
gale*. As early as 1917, however, these gropings were to lead
to a remarkable and precocious triumph.

Browsing in a Paris bookshop, he came upon a volume
of verse quaintly entitled *Les Poésies de Makoko Kangourou*.
These poems, supposedly written by a negro from Liberia,
were a deliberate hoax. Negro art was the fashion of the
day and, unconcerned with their authenticity, Poulenc
maliciously decided to set the bogus poem *Honoloulou*:

> Honoloulou, poti lama!
> Honoloulou, Honoloulou,
> Kati moko, mosi bolou
> Ratakou sira, polama!

The three verses of this poem were used for a vocal
interlude which formed the central section of the *Rapsodie
Nègre*. This spontaneous work for baritone, piano, string
quartet, flute and clarinet is in five movements and was
first given on December 11th, 1917, at one of a series of
memorable concerts of contemporary music organised by
Jeanne Bathori at the Théâtre du Vieux-Colombier. At the
last moment the baritone was so terrified of his part that he
refused to sing, whereupon the young composer himself
promptly replaced him. The youthful charm of the work,
the musical instrumentation and the streak of genuine

humour in Poulenc made an immediate impact. It was a
roaring success, and overnight the career of the eighteen-
year-old composer was launched. The same success
marked a repeat performance of the *Rapsodie Nègre*. The
inquiring mind of Diaghilev toyed with the idea of Poulenc
writing a ballet, which he eventually did. Stravinsky was
sufficiently impressed to introduce him to his London
publishers, Chester's, who brought out the *Rapsodie Nègre*
and the *Mouvements perpétuels*, and Ravel, too, admired his
precocious gifts, emphasising, however, the necessity for
training.

In January, 1918, Poulenc was called up for military
service and was sent to Vincennes where he remained until
July. He was then dispatched to the front, in the Vosges,
where he served in an anti-aircraft unit. In October he was
at Saint-Martin-sur-le-Pré, near Châlon, and in December
at the anti-aircraft school at Pont-sur-Seine. In July, 1919,
he was drafted to the Ministry of Aviation as a typist and
stayed there for over two years, until October, 1921, when
he was demobilised. He had, however, not forsaken composition in the course of his military duties. The *Mouvements
perpétuels* and the Sonata for piano duet were written at the
piano of the local elementary school at Saint-Martin-sur-
le-Pré.

The world fame of the *Mouvements perpétuels*, which
Ricardo Viñès first performed in 1919 at one of a series of
concerts called *Lyre et Palette*, has long been an accepted
fact. The qualities of these three short pieces are self-evident.
Spontaneous and most attractively melodious, they display,
in the manner of Satie, a genre of the eighteenth-century

Le Grand Coteau, Poulenc's home at Noizay in the Touraine

Paul Eluard (above) and
Guillaume Apollinaire:
drawings by Picasso

harpsichord composers tastefully spiced with the still new twentieth-century notions of dissonance.

Undeservedly, the Sonata for piano duet has not yet made this same appeal. It is worth quoting Ernest Ansermet's appraisement when this work was published by Chester's in 1919: 'I do not wish to hide my pleasure in seeing this music which strikes me as the most genuine and alive music that France has recently produced. Each of the three short movements establishes new harmonic boundaries without, however, any unnecessary embroidery. Using the simplest of musical devices and built on an equally simple though by no means unattractive pattern, the three movements do, in fact, amount to a Sonata in the sense that Debussy's *Pour le piano* and the earliest examples of the form may be considered Sonatas. Both harmonically and melodically they are very much to the point, showing a thoughtful knowledge of Stravinsky but unmistakably French in spirit: they reveal something of the subtlety of Ravel, the joviality of Satie, particularly in the Finale, and occasionally a spirit of abandon (in the sixth bar of the movement entitled *Rustique*) that recalls Chabrier. The somewhat child-like impression of these fresh and spontaneous pieces, of which the best seems to be the *Rustique*, is exactly what we are looking for in the music of youth. . . . [Poulenc] is one of the most attractive personalities in the new music of our time.' The same approachable qualities mark the excellently written Sonata for two clarinets (in B flat and A) of the same year (1918).

The first songs were written at Pont-sur-Seine in February, 1919. A new edition of *Le Bestiaire* by Guillaume Apollinaire,

C

illustrated with wood-cuts by Raoul Dufy, had been brought
out by the Editions de la Sirène and was sent to Poulenc by
Adrienne Monnier. He had in fact recently been introduced
to Apollinaire by Valentine Hugo. He learnt several of the
poems by heart and set twelve of them to music at the piano
of a country house. Acting on Auric's advice he published
only six, *Le Dromadaire*, *La Chèvre du Tibet*, *La Sauterelle*,
Le Dauphin, *L'Ecrevisse* and *La Carpe*.

These short songs, which were to be sung without a
break, quickly made their mark. Again the melodic gifts of
the youthful composer were held to be immediately striking.
Like the Chinese Hai-kai, these miniatures were evidence of
a degree of intimacy between musician and poet that was to
deepen in the later settings of Apollinaire. Indeed, with
Paul Eluard, Guillaume Apollinaire became the poet with
whom Poulenc was completely identified. The little songs
of *Le Bestiaire* had, according to Marie Laurencin, 'the very
sound of Apollinaire's voice'. Yet despite the miniature
scale, *Le Bestiaire* is the work of a serious mind not intent, as
one might be led to suppose, on any expression of clownish-
ness or irony. Nor are they a counterpart of Jules Renard's
subtly humorous *Histoires Naturelles* as set to music by Ravel.
The sixth song, *La Carpe*, is an early example of the composer's purely lyrical inspiration. The accompaniment,
usually heard in the piano arrangement, was originally
scored for flute, clarinet, bassoon and string quartet.

*   *   *

Following this master-stroke, Poulenc set to music round
about this time *Cocardes*, the 'three popular songs' on poems

of Jean Cocteau entitled *Miel de Narbonne, Bonne d'enfant*
and *Enfant de troupe*. The composer acknowledges a reflection in them of some of Stravinsky's ideas on orchestration
and also of that touch of irony in the patriotic works of
Roger de la Fresnaye. The accompaniment, like that of *Le
Bestiaire*, was originally written for a small instrumental
ensemble (violin, cornet, trombone, bass drum and triangle)
the scoring of which was revised in 1939.

Although of the same period as *Le Bestiaire*, these three
ironic imitations of popular songs are altogether different in
outlook and style. Isolated words in these humorous
juxtapositions of Cocteau hop about, so it seemed to the
composer, 'like birds from tree to tree':

> Morceau pour piston seul
> Polka
> Caramels mous, bonbons acidulés
> Pastilles de menthe
> Entracte
> L'odeur en
> Beau gibier de satin tué par le tambour
> Hambourg
> Bock
> Sirop de framboise
> Oiseleur de ses propres mains
> Intermède uniforme bleu
> Le trapèze.[1]

1   Piece for solo cornet   Peppermints
    Polka   Interval
    Soft caramels, acid drops   The smell of

On these enigmatic poems composed of words liberated, as it were, from their normal association and conveying therefore an entirely different spirit from the verse of Apollinaire, Poulenc wrote a series of biting sarcastic pieces. Thematic development has no place in this almost reproachful music, and in the assembling of these glinting chips Poulenc was, in a sense, served by his very lack of experience. They recall the figure of Erik Satie, rather than Stravinsky, and particularly the music of *Parade* with its echoes of contemporary music-hall and circus tunes behind which there lurked, for these composers, a note of affecting sentimentality. In *Enfant de troupe*, the best of the three songs forming *Cocardes*, there are two bars reproducing some kind of barrel-organ refrain leading directly into a trumpet fanfare reminiscent of Bastille Day celebrations. Nevertheless a hint may be discovered, too, in the slow section of the second song, *Bonne d'enfant*, of Poulenc's naturally melodious and traditional manner, later illustrated in the *Aubade* and the *Concert champêtre*.

The particular interest of these three songs, however, lies in their curious period value: they belong to the period of Jean Cocteau's *Le Coq et l'Arlequin* (1918) and the ballet *Parade*, the joint work of Satie, Cocteau and Picasso, which had set alight a traditional Paris theatrical scandal at its first performance by the Russian Ballet on May 18th, 1917.

The scathing manifesto of *Le Coq et l'Arlequin*, written in

Fine game in satin killed by a drum
Hamburg
Glass of beer
Raspberry Syrup

The bird-catcher with his own hands
Intermezzo blue uniforms
Trapeze act.

Cocteau's paradoxical and lapidary style, was calculated to shatter what seemed to be the alarming hold of the Wagnerian musical religion. Cocteau believed there was to be music other than that which compelled adoring listeners to bury their heads in their hands. 'In London Wagner is performed,' he notes, 'in Paris he is secretly regretted.' And he launches his attack in these terms: 'Certain long works are short. Length, however, in Wagner, is an essential feature of his work, for the reason that ennui is used by this musical god as a convenient drug to stupefy his faithful followers.' The Parisian vogue of Moussorgsky and Rimsky-Korsakov similarly comes under fire; and so does much woolly music written in imitation of Debussy. He champions the primitive cause, on the other hand, of *Le Sacre du Printemps*, and the chaste simplicity of Erik Satie. Excessive refinement and superfluous ornament were anathema. 'Impressionist ears were struck by the poverty of the orchestration of *Parade*, for the reason that Satie had refrained from using any kind of instrumental sauce.' He speaks of Satie as an 'orphan of music, his mind open to dreams, who will show a way to the young composers burdened by the beauties of Impressionist polyphony'.

The younger figures were in fact thinking on these lines, and naturally rallied to the cause of *Parade* and also to Satie himself, who had achieved celebrity overnight. A cellist, Félix Delgrange, took the new composers of the day under his wing and organised concerts of their works in a humble studio in the Rue Huyghens in Montparnasse. Darius Milhaud recalls the rows of primitive benches and the unbreathable smoke in this out-of-the-way studio crammed

with the forward-looking figures of the day. The new
works were given by the pianists Ricardo Viñès, Juliette
Mecrovitch and Marcelle Meyer, the singers Jeanne Bathori
and Pierre Bertin, the violinist Hélène Jourdan-Morhange
and the Capelle Quartet. Delgrange also organised a concert
performance of *Parade* at this studio which was now a
resounding success. Works of Satie were regularly given
alongside those of the new generation, namely Georges
Auric, Darius Milhaud, Arthur Honegger, Germaine
Tailleferre, Roland Manuel, Louis Durey and Francis
Poulenc, some of them only just finished or, in fact, not
even ready. In her book *Mes amis musiciens*, Hélène Jourdan-
Morhange speaks of an unpublished piano and violin sonata
of Poulenc, dedicated to her, but of which the composer
had not found the time to complete the piano part. 'We
played only the first two movements which were very
lovely. . . . It seemed that this young band had the one idea
of rushing headlong in a direction that offered them escape
from the vampires of a past age.'

The famous *Groupe des Six* came into being from these
Delgrange concerts. After one of the concerts the critic
Henri Collet wrote two articles in *Comoedia*, the first
entitled 'The Five Russians, the Six Frenchmen and Satie',
the second 'The Six Frenchmen'. 'In completely arbitrary
fashion,' notes Darius Milhaud, 'Henri Collet chose the
names of six composers, Auric, Durey, Honegger, Poulenc,
Tailleferre and myself, for no other reason than that we
knew each other, that we were friends and were represented
in the same programmes, but without the slightest concern
for our different attitudes and our different natures. Auric

and Poulenc followed the ideas of Cocteau, Honegger was a product of German Romanticism and my leanings were towards a Mediterranean lyrical art. . . . Collet's article made such a wide impression that the *Groupe des Six* had come into being.'

The six members gracefully accepted this label which had thus been affixed to them after the fashion of the famous Russian 'Great Five' (Balakirev, Borodin, Cui, Moussorgsky and Rimsky-Korsakov). It is well known that the Russians had a common musical ideal, whereas the young Frenchmen were bound only by the personal friendships between them and such very general notions as the need, commonly shared, to reinstate the claims of a less pretentious type of music in opposition to the overwhelming impact of Wagner, the mists that lingered in the wake of Debussy and the dogmatic theories preached by Vincent d'Indy at the Schola Cantorum.

Since the Paris world had been told of the existence of the *Groupe des Six*, it was not long before there followed a series of *Concerts des Six*. The first was devoted to works by the six members, and the second to works by their foreign contemporaries, Lord Berners, Alfredo Casella, Arthur Lourié, Arnold Schoenberg and Béla Bartók (the last two were greatly admired). Similar concerts were given abroad, the first of which was in Belgium.

The six composers naturally became more and more closely associated on a purely friendly plane. 'We used to meet regularly at my home every Saturday evening over a period of two years,' Milhaud recalls in his *Notes sans Musique*. 'Paul Morand would make cocktails and then we went off to a little restaurant at the top of the Rue Blanche.

This restaurant, "Le Petit Bessonneau", was so tiny that once the Saturday visitors had crowded in there was not a seat left. Apart from ourselves, others who came were the pianists Marcelle Meyer, Juliette Mecrovitch and Andrée Vaurabourg (the fiancée of Arthur Honegger), the Russian singer Koubitzky, the painters Marie Laurencin, Irène Lagut, Valentine Gross (the fiancée of Jean Hugo) and Guy-Pierre Fauconnet, and the writers Lucien Daudet and Raymond Radiguet, a young poet introduced to our circle by Cocteau. After dinner we used to roam through the Montmartre fairgrounds, delighted by the old-fashioned roundabouts, the strange shops, quaint attractions such as the Daughter of Mars, the rifle ranges and lotteries, the menageries and the din from the barrel-organs with their perforated rolls that seemed to blare out simultaneously every tune and ditty to be heard at that time at the Paris music-halls and revues. Sometimes we went to the Cirque de Médrano to see the acts of the Fratellinis, full of a sense of poetry that was worthy of the Commedia dell'Arte. Eventually we returned to my home. The poets read their verse and we played our latest works. Some of them, Auric's *Adieu New York*, Poulenc's *Cocardes* and my *Boeuf sur le Toit*, were gone over again and again. We required Poulenc to play his *Cocardes* unfailingly every Saturday, which he did in the sweetest manner. Many fruitful artistic collaborations may be traced back to these happy gatherings, and also certain works illustrating what amounted to the new music-hall aesthetic.'

A memorable evening of works of these music-hall associations was February 21st, 1920, when new works of

Milhaud, Poulenc and Satie were given before a privately
invited audience at the Comédie des Champs-Elysées. They
were Milhaud's *Boeuf sur le Toit*, with scenery by Raoul
Dufy and a plot devised by Jean Cocteau, in which the
principal parts were taken by clowns from the Cirque de
Médrano and the Fratellinis; Satie's three little *Pièces
Montées*, specially written for the occasion; and Poulenc's
Cocardes, sung in public for the first time, by the tenor
Koubitzky. Count Etienne de Beaumont disposed of all the
boxes well ahead of time and at a high figure. The Shah of
Persia paid ten thousand francs for a box above the stage
from where nothing could be seen, though he was himself
in view of the entire audience. The success of the evening
was tremendous, marking the emergence of the new music-
hall aesthetic which was indiscriminately applied to all the
members of the *Groupe des Six*. The sponsorship of Satie,
considered at that time a fraud, was not the least important
cause of *Les Six* acquiring the standing of a comical band
not to be taken too seriously.

To counter this unsophisticated and false view, the group
published that year a journal first called *Le Coq* and, by the
time of its second number, *Le Coq Parisien*, got up in the
form of a placard. This was a most scathing sheet, brimming
over with youthful enthusiasm, having no truck with any
kind of dogmatic theory, but forceful and challenging.
'Ravel refuses the Legion of Honour but his entire musical
work accepts it,' wrote Erik Satie. It was he too, in a
declaration entitled 'No Barracks Here', who denounced
any idea of a Satie *École*: 'I have never attacked Debussy.
My worry is the Debussysts. There can be no such thing as

Satisme; if there were, I should be hostile to it. In art there must be no slavery. I have always striven, by the form and content of each new work, to put followers off the scent. This is the only means for an artist not to turn himself into a *chef d'école*, that is to say a mere pawn.'

In the ensuing polemics, Jean Cocteau wrote a sharp reply to Paul Souday who had described *Le Coq* as the official organ of Cubism. '*Le Coq* is the organ of no school. It is a paper in which six musicians of different outlook but united by friendly bonds express their opinions. . . . Poets and painters who feel at one with them are similarly represented. . . . Simply because an opinion expressed by one may not meet with the approval of another does not mean that such very acceptable disagreements can possibly sow discord.' Georges Auric summed up the situation by declaring that once the cause had been won of the movement against the over-refinements of Debussyism, the dangers of modernism, its equally undesirable antidote, were still to be overcome. On what was the plebeian appeal of the circus, the music-hall and the Montmartre fairground based? Melody was the key of this appeal. The raw music of the fairgrounds would have a salutary effect. No matter if it obliterated the lingering impressions of Debussyism or the grace of Maurice Ravel. Here was where talents were likely to be dangerously stifled. Awakened in time, composers may see the danger for what it is. In *Daphnis and Chloe* Ravel uses a wind-machine; composers may one day use with equal effect a machine to scatter the wind.

Jazz is found to be enchanting. . . . But today, and this is a sign of the weariness of the period, nationalism has had to be re-invented. Peering further into the problem, Auric admits having been stimulated by jazz, and this being so, not another note of it should be heard. Auric's *Fox-trot* was therefore entitled *Adieu New York*. The 'Latest News' of *Le Coq* announced 'the foundation of an Anti-Modern League—a return to poetry—disappearance of the skyscraper—reappearance of the rose'. Skyscrapers were, however, to remain. *Le Coq* came to an end with its fourth number.

On June 18th, 1921, was given the only joint work of *Les Six* (with the exception of Louis Durey who had seceded). This was *Les Mariés de la Tour Eiffel*, produced by the Swedish Ballet of Rolf de Maré at the Théâtre des Champs-Elysées.

'Was this a ballet?' asked Jean Cocteau in the journal *La Danse* (June, 1921). 'No. A play? No. A revue? No. A tragedy? Still less. It represented a sort of secret marriage between the idea of the tragedy of antiquity and the latest conception of a revue.' Cocteau had himself devised the scenario. In spirit *Les Mariés de la Tour Eiffel* purported to illustrate a conception of 'poetry *of* the theatre' as opposed to 'poetry *at* the theatre'. In *Les Feuilles Libres* (February, 1922), Raymond Radiguet wrote: 'In the theatre, the greatest poets have always made the mistake of embellishing their work with poetic images which merely hold up the interest and the dramatic action. The language here is not a language of imagery, but the play itself.' By means of the scenery and costumes of Irène Lagut, which had been inspired by the remarkable talent of the poet Jean Hugo, such common sights as the Eiffel Tower, cyclists and photographers were displayed, not as the common phenomena they were usually considered to be, but endowed with a refreshing, child-like sense of poetry. Georges Auric wrote a tart, jovial Overture evoking Paris street scenes on Bastille Day, and three Ritornelles; Poulenc, 'The Dance of a bathing girl at Tourville' (a deliberately comic polka) and an hilarious piece called 'The General's Speech'; Germaine Tailleferre, 'The Waltz of the Telegrams' and a Quadrille; Milhaud, a facetious Nuptial March and a 'Fugue of the Massacre of a Wedding'; and finally Honegger, a joyous 'Funeral March of the General'. This last was the only piece to be taken seriously. 'In the "Funeral March",' Cocteau wrote, 'Arthur Honegger took it upon himself to parody what the historians solemnly refer to as "Music". It need hardly be said that they all fell into the trap. No sooner were the opening themes heard than their long ears stood up. . . . Not one of the critics recognised that the bass was the Waltz from *Faust*.'

The first performance of *Les Mariés de la Tour Eiffel* was the scene of another unforgettable hullabaloo. The fall of the curtain brought all manner of cat-calls and insults. Marking the climax of the activities of *Les Six* as a group, *Les Mariés de la Tour Eiffel* represents also the end of the group's communal existence. Louis Durey, on the pretext of ill-health, had refused to co-operate. The fact is, as we have seen, that had there not been the catch-phrase of Henri Collet, the *Groupe des Six* would never have come into existence. Poulenc has himself stated that 'the diversity of our musical ideals, our likes and dislikes precluded a common

aesthetic. What could be more dissimilar than the work of
Honegger and the work of Auric? Milhaud admired
Magnard, but I didn't; neither of us was fond of the music
of Florent Schmitt respected, however, by Honegger.
Honegger, on the other hand, really despised Satie whom
Auric, Milhaud and myself adored.' In the course of the
year that he collaborated with his friends on *Les Mariés de la
Tour Eiffel*, Honegger wrote his *Horace Victorieux* and *King
David*. He was following a way of his own which, in fact,
was what each of *Les Six* was now to do.

* 　 * 　 *

During his early boyhood days at school, Francis Poulenc's
aim had been to study at the Paris Conservatoire. But his
father would have none of it: he insisted on his son pursuing
his normal school studies at the Lycée Condorcet. After *Les
Mariés de la Tour Eiffel*, by which time he had completed
his military service, the young composer, who had now
acquired a degree of celebrity, saw clearly enough that he
should act on Ravel's admonition to lay a solid technical
grounding. His quick successes had not left him intoxicated,
and on the advice of Darius Milhaud he became a private
pupil of the admirable teacher, Charles Koechlin, who was
also an interesting composer though his works are still
relatively unknown. His period of study with Koechlin
extended from 1921 to 1924.

Koechlin realised immediately that his pupil was in no
way gifted for counterpoint and consequently did not
burden him with the usual contrapuntal exercises. His

weekly exercises consisted of chorales, in the form of free four-part harmonisations, on themes of Bach; and it was from these that he gradually acquired the subtle art of *a capella* writing.

In the meantime his creative work continued: two piano works were written in 1920—the three-movement Suite in C major dedicated to Viñès and very reminiscent of Satie, and the Five Impromptus dedicated to Marcelle Meyer. These were unpretentious works, well carried off, but not the match, in spontaneity, of the *Mouvements perpétuels*. Technical shortcomings were beginning to show. They were, however, better than the ten *Promenades* of 1921, rather more complex pieces in which the composer's talents lose their hold. Poulenc becomes himself again in the two Sonatas, one for clarinet and bassoon, the other for horn, trumpet and trombone, of 1922. Characteristically tart and sentimental, they are well conceived for these wind instruments and resemble the Sonata for two clarinets which belongs to the same period as the *Mouvements perpétuels*. Another work is the incidental music for the one-act comedy by Jean Cocteau and Raymond Radiguet, *Le Gendarme Incompris*. This play, in which some lines of Mallarmé spoken by a comic policeman in his normal manner of speech went unrecognised, was performed in May, 1921, at the Théâtre des Mathurins, in the course of an avant-garde evening organised by Pierre Bertin. Milhaud has expressed regret that Poulenc should have refused to allow any further performance of what struck him as a most delightful work.

In 1918, while the war was still being fought, the *Groupe des Six* had collectively sent a 'Greeting to Arnold Schoenberg', whom they had recognised as a great contemporary master. Once the war was over, Milhaud and Poulenc were anxious to develop their contacts with the Austrian musical world, and they accordingly left for Central Europe together with Marya Freund who had given the first French performance of Schoenberg's *Pierrot Lunaire*.

In Vienna they were received at the home of Gustav Mahler's widow, at that time the brilliant centre of Austrian musical life, where they met Alban Berg, whom they greatly admired, and Anton Webern.

At the request of Frau Mahler they organised two performances of *Pierrot Lunaire* in Vienna, one conducted by Schoenberg and sung by Erika Wagner, the other conducted by Milhaud (who, since the end of the war, had given the work several times in Paris and Brussels) with Marya Freund. 'It was a wonderful experience,' Milhaud recalls. 'In Schoenberg's reading the chromaticism of the work was emphasised with more harshness and frenzy, whereas I attempted to bring out the more sensitive and subtle aspects. Erika Wagner declaimed the German text in rasping tones, but was less concerned with the actual notes than Marya Freund who perhaps adhered to them too closely. I at once realised that there could be no solution of this particular vocal problem.'

They were later to see Schoenberg at his home at Mödling near Vienna, when the two French composers played their works to him at the piano. Schoenberg spoke at length of his own works, particularly his operas *Die Glückliche Hand* and *Erwartung* of which Milhaud had bought the scores. Shortly after his visit to Mödling, Poulenc fell ill and was urgently operated on for an abscess on the throat. An act of particular kindness, remembered with gratitude, was the gift of a pot of jam, a rare delicacy in those days of near-famine, from Egon Wellesz.

The following year Milhaud and Poulenc set out together on another journey abroad, this time to Italy. Alfredo Casella had wanted to offer them an engagement at one of the Santa Cecilia concerts, but the revolutionary reputation of Les Six told against them. A private concert was given by the two composers at the home of Count Lovatelli.

Rome was an enchantment. Claude Delvincourt, holder of the Prix de Rome, invited them to the Villa Medici, and they also met in Rome the younger Italian composers, Gianfrancesco Malipiero, Mario Labrocca and Vittorio Rieti, the last a frequent visitor to Paris where he became largely assimilated. Around Rome they visited Tivoli, Frascati and the Villa d'Este, and went on to Naples and Sicily.

No new works were brought back from Italy by Milhaud, but Poulenc was inspired at this time to write his piano suite *Napoli*. Not published until 1925, this three-movement suite has found favour with several of the outstanding pianists of today, among them Rubinstein and Arrau—unaccountably, for it must be put down, along with the *Promenades*, as one of the composer's least successful pianistic achievements.

A turning-point in Poulenc's career came in 1923 with the composition of the ballet *Les Biches*, his first large-scale work and still one of the most striking in his output. The youthful

'Les Six' by Jean Cocteau: Germaine Tailleferre, Louis
Durey, Georges Auric, Francis Poulenc, Darius Milhaud
and Arthur Honegger. Jean Cocteau is in the centre

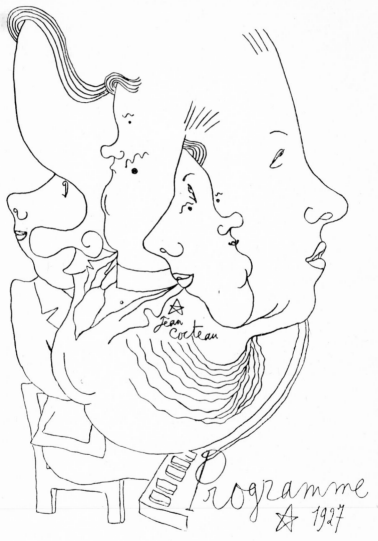

Francis Poulenc and Georges Auric by Jean Cocteau

composer who had long been a fervent admirer of the
Russian Ballet was enchanted with the commission from
Diaghilev. The suggestion put to Poulenc was for a modern
equivalent of *Les Sylphides*. His own idea, he said, was 'of a
sort of contemporary version of the *Fêtes galantes* in which,
as in certain pictures of Watteau, anything one wishes may
be seen or imagined'.

The scenario was practically non-existent. Sixteen
exquisite young females appear in a large drawing-room
grouped around a single piece of furniture, an enormous
couch. Three strapping young athletic figures, dressed as
oarsmen, play the cocks among the hens. The various set
dances, *pas de deux*, *pas de trois* and group figures, were
devised to illustrate much subtle by-play, and occasionally
a hidden allusion: one of the *pas de deux*, performed by two
danseuses, might have been entitled *Les deux amies* in illustration of the scene between Albertine and a girl-friend at
Balbec in Proust. It is a ballet conceived in celebration of
pure pleasure—pleasure, that is to say, unaffected by pangs
of conscience: the purity of innocence is not a quality of
these *biches* of Poulenc's creation (the word has the double,
though associated, meaning of 'hind', the female of deer,
and 'darling').

Since there is no clear-cut scenario, the score is not bound
to follow any kind of anecdotal pattern, nor is it built on the
model of a symmetrical form. It is a suite of dances, each
complete in itself, of which the titles are *Ouverture*, *Rondeau*,
Chanson dansée, *Adagietto*, *Jeu*, *Mazurka*, *Andantino*, *Petite
chanson dansée* and *Final*. Some of them recall the style of the
medieval *chansons dansées* (the words but not the music of

D

which being taken from French folk-lore), and in these the dancers on the stage give expression to the words of the singers in the orchestra pit. These sections of *Les Biches*, it is worth noting, form Poulenc's first choral work.

'Exquisite' is the word that must describe the music of *Les Biches*—in the word's precise and original sense. Freedom is there, but not a freedom that stirs the depths or that includes any suggestion of gravity.

With its ironic and slightly rakish twists, its thoroughly traditional elegance of musical thought, it goes straight to the point, its one aim being to bring delight. It has nothing stilted, nor can one detect pretence. It is graceful, but it does not sink to a level of insipidity or mere prettiness. A tenderness of sentiment is proclaimed (notably in the *Adagietto*), but it is a tenderness that does not languish. Underlying the line-drawing precision of its contours is a subtle, sinewy strength. A disciplined musical mind lies behind the apparent ease and freedom. Its impulsiveness, bringing with it (in the *Rag-Mazurka* and the *Final*) an abruptly repressed display of exuberance, is the impulsiveness of youth, as indeed is its open freshness of spirit and also a note of shyness. This beautifully clear score is not music bent on making out-of-the-way allusions; it makes straight for its goal. It is a score irresistibly evoking the art of Domenico Scarlatti.

Granted that it may all be nothing more than a game, but it is still a very clever game—of the mind and of the heart. An irresistible gaiety and grace emanate from this unconstrained ballet score, in which there is more of the composer's inner self than might appear. Occasionally the sensitive composer hides behind his mask—and his music at these moments is flooded with some sort of heartfelt melancholy.

The question arises as to whether Poulenc uses an original musical language in *Les Biches*. This is a question that seemed to have very much worried the critics of 1924. The composer was the first to admit that the *Adagietto* was suggested by a Variation from Tchaikovsky's *Sleeping Beauty*, as in fact he has also admitted the influence of Stravinsky's *Pulcinella* and *Mavra*. Other echoes of Stravinsky are the strident brass fanfares in the *Chanson dansée* and the syncopated rhythms of the *Rag-Mazurka*. But these derivative questions have no longer the interest they once had: it is a work that is Poulenc's own. In a shrewd appraisement that appeared in *La Revue musicale*, Boris de Schloezer admitted traces of Mozart, Stravinsky and even Beethoven, but went on to draw a valid distinction between plagiarism and a perfectly legitimate appropriation of stylistic elements which, in *Les Biches*, invariably acquired something of the composer's individuality.

Admirable counterparts of the score were provided by the choreography of Nijinska and the scenery and costumes of Marie Laurencin. Laurencin's roses and pale blues bordered on but managed just not to melt into sentimentality; attitudes struck in Nijinska's choreography were similarly conceived as a tight-rope feat of discrimination. The tip-toe entry in the *Adagietto* of Vera Nemtchinova, dressed in a short blue velvet jacket, her legs sheathed in white, was sensational. Remembering Stendhal's particular understanding of the word 'sublime', Jean Cocteau in *La Revue de*

Paris declared that this entry of Nemtchinova was a true illustration of what Stendhal meant by the word (in a sense, as he said, beyond the appreciation of the Wagnerians). 'When this sweet little lady tip-toes on to the stage from the wings,' he went on, 'the sight of those beautiful long legs, of her ever so short tight-fitting jacket, and of her white-gloved right hand by the side of her cheek suggesting a military salute bring a flutter to the heart—if indeed a beat is not missed. Faultless taste marked her merging of novel and classical steps.'

Les Biches was first given at the Théâtre de Monte-Carlo on January 6th, 1924, and in Paris on May 26th of the same year, under the direction of André Messager. On both occasions it had a triumphant reception. Louis Laloy, who hailed the work as an outstanding event, had a mind to reserve some of his applause for the understanding and appreciative public. Another distinguished critic, Henry Malherbe, similarly emphasised its original qualities.

The academically-minded Adolphe Boschot, on the other hand, saw in it nothing more than overblown music-hall tunes which he considered to be caricatures. Alone, Emile Vuillermoz found the score 'monotonous'. It was pleasing, he added, but banal, 'failing to achieve any of the lightness of effect which was its aim'—a curious verdict on this agile, quicksilver score which over the years has lost nothing of its original appeal.

One week after *Les Biches*, the production of Georges Auric's ballet *Les Fâcheux* was a similar triumph. The ardent champion of the two composers was Debussy's great friend, Louis Laloy, who had written enthusiastic articles on their

ballets. This new friendship of the enthusiastic Laloy was to
have a deadly effect on their relations with Erik Satie. Satie
had gone to Monte Carlo for the first performances. A
sworn enemy of Laloy, he had taken umbrage at Laloy's
growing friendship for the two young composers. On his
return to Paris he sent the following post-card to Poulenc.

Monsieur Francis Poulenc,
Hôtel des Princes,
Monte Carlo,
Monaco.   Friday, January 11th, 1924
    Dear Friend: Good day—and how goes it? Bravo again and again
for *Les Biches*—Allow me to suggest to you that you do not make too
many advances to Sire (Sawyer) [sieur (scieur)] L.L. . . . Yes. Beware
of this fellow. Yes. . . . Don't forget that you are a thousand times
superior to him. YES. Greetings.
                                                          E.S.

The implied warning in these lines was soon to assume
ugly proportions, particularly in regard to Satie's connec-
tions with Auric. Taking as an excuse a not altogether
laudatory article written by Auric in *Les Nouvelles Littéraires*
on Satie's *Mercure*, Satie wrote the following lines in the
Revue '391', edited by the painter Picabia:
'Very well, my little friend, let him go on. Let him
Laloy himself as much as he likes. Then we'll see what we
shall see.
'What is my crime? I don't like his patched-up, tricked-
out *Fâcheux*. Those who tell me that this late friend of mine
is nothing more than an old flat-foot are overstating his
merits; he is nothing more than an Auric (Georges)—which
is more than enough for a man, if he is a man, on his own.'
Auric retaliated, not without understandable bitterness.

At that period Auric and Poulenc used to play poker regularly every week with Arthur Honegger and the singer Claire Croiza. One morning Poulenc went to a shop called the *Nain Bleu* in the Rue du Faubourg St Honoré to buy some cards. He noticed in the shop a child's rattle to which was affixed a bearded head unmistakably suggesting the head of Satie. Auric proceeded to buy it and, with Poulenc's full approval, dispatched it to the venerable Satie. This, in view of an unyielding, suspicious and tetchy aspect of Satie's character, causing him to break with all his friends (notably, after *Parade*, with Debussy), inevitably resulted in a rupture. Debussy, at death's door, weary and possibly somewhat embittered by the growing renown of his old friend, had given Satie no sign. Stung by this silence, Satie wrote Debussy an insulting letter. Laloy recalls that it was received by Debussy on his death-bed. 'His trembling hands ran over the sheets and seized the letter which was abruptly torn to pieces. "Pardon," he muttered, like a child about to be scolded and with tears in his eyes.'

Satie never forgave Auric and Poulenc for sending him the rattle. When, shortly before his death, their mutual friend Raymonde Linassier tried to bring about a reconciliation, Satie replied in terms of mingled pride and wretchedness but which nevertheless command respect. 'What can be the use of seeing them again? Debussy himself died without my seeing him again.'

II
(1925 - 1938)
Cinq Poèmes de Ronsard to the Organ Concerto

In 1925, Poulenc produced the first songs he had written for six years. These were the *Cinq Poèmes de Ronsard*, consisting of *Attributs*, *Le Tombeau*, *Ballet*, *Je n'ai plus que les os* and *A Son page*. They were first performed by Suzanne Peignot and received an enthusiastic press. André Schaeffner praised the marriage of music and poetry, and André George maintained that Poulenc had discovered the bridge that leads from Ronsard to the present day.

The composer himself, however, has since become severely critical of these early Ronsard songs, attractively brought out with an admirable cover by Picasso. Despite many pleasing aspects, one cannot deny an artificial and rather heavily ornate impression. Possibly under the influence of his master Koechlin, the texture, as in the *Promenades* for piano, becomes unnecessarily thickened. Auric's perspicacious comments were welcome. The composer's true manner, Auric found, was evident only in the beginning of the first song and the end of the last. Contrary to a widely expressed opinion, Poulenc, he maintained, had no affinity with the earlier French poets. Apollinaire, he urged, should be the poet of his choice, also Max Jacob, Eluard and Reverdy.

In the meantime, a new cycle was embarked upon.

The sprightly *Chansons gaillardes*, on anonymous eighteenth-century poems, ring a tauntingly seductive note with praise of wine, women and song shot through with racy allusions. The eight short songs of this cycle are entitled *La Maîtresse volage, Chanson à boire, Madrigal, Invocation aux Parques, Couplets bachiques, L'Offrande, La belle Jeunesse* and *Sérénade*. Only one, *Invocation aux Parques*, the text of which, a tribute to fidelity, may possibly be by Racine, stands in contrast to the high-spirited mood.

The *Chansons gaillardes* mark the composer's mastery of the French *Mélodie*. Without the slightest suggestion of false modesty, his Gallic mind pierces the heart of the pithy rhymes which are thus free to make their full impact in Poulenc's shamelessly beautiful settings. Not only are the vocal lines more distinctive, but the piano accompaniments are likewise resourceful, displaying in *La belle Jeunesse* and *Les Couplets Bachiques* a remarkable lightness of touch and sense of vivacity. The cycle was first given at a concert of the works of Poulenc and Auric at the Salle des Agriculteurs on 2 May 1926. The unknown singer who carried them off with such brilliant success was Pierre Bernac, from whom the name of Poulenc was soon to be inseparable.

At the same concert, the first performance was given of the Trio for piano, oboe and bassoon, Poulenc's first major achievement in the sphere of chamber music. Milhaud's first encounter with Poulenc had reminded him of the *mot* of Vincent d'Indy: 'La musique française deviendra ce que le prochain musicien de génie voudra qu'elle soit'; and he was inclined to think that, following the Impressionist period, a new phase would be marked by the clear-cut art of Poulenc which had reverted to the ideals of Scarlatti and of Mozart. This prediction, inspired by the *Bestiaire* and the *Mouvements Perpétuels*, was in fact justified by the much more assured manner of the Trio.

A short introduction, grave or wry in mood—one is never quite sure—opens the first of the three movements and leads to a wittily written *Presto* section, brilliantly carried off but not without a show of mock sentimentality. The chaste opening theme of the *Andante* is first given to the piano. It is presently passed to the wind instruments, the character of the oboe being particularly apt to convey its lyrical purity. The ironic character of the oboe, on the other hand, is artfully brought out in the final swift-moving *Rondo*, made to race to its goal, amusingly contrived as a sudden and unexpected stop. Something of the spirit of Mozart persists in this youthful, concise work: it is indeed music in which the claims of the mind and the heart are adjusted with surprising skill. Nor are certain technical aspects of the work less astonishing. Poulenc had set himself the unusual problem of combining the percussive piano with two wind instruments. Pictorially, one is sometimes reminded of a chase, sometimes of a dialogue. Normally, however, the main musical discourse is entrusted to the piano, while the bassoon is relegated to the rôle of a discreet commentator and the oboe is allowed to intensify the more lyrical flights. The very heart of Poulenc is in this adroit little work, written now over thirty years ago.

The *Airs Chantés* (1927-8) consist of four songs, *Air romantique*, *Air champêtre*, *Air grave* and *Air vif*, on poems of Jean Moréas. These, again, were to be roundly condemned by the composer. 'I am constantly astonished,' Poulenc has himself written in his *Journal de mes Mélodies*, 'at ever having thought of writing these songs. I have no gift for paradox— an expression of paradox in music requires the mastery of a Ravel. The fact is that I loathe these poems of Moréas and I chose them for this very reason, namely that I thought they deserved to be torn to shreds. In the *Air champêtre* I under-lined a certain aspect of the prosody. Have I been punished for such vandalism? I fear I have, for this unlikeable song has won ill-deserved success. The *Air grave* is surely the worst of my songs, conventional in the extreme. As for the joyous explosion which is the *Air vif*, this has turned out to be a typical example of meretricious success. The outcome of all this is that I simply turned away from writing songs alto-gether for a long time to come.'

Clearly, there was nothing in Poulenc's nature that could be readily attuned to the coldly-calculated aspirations of Jean Moréas, the French symbolist poet of Greek origin who followed the letter rather than the spirit of the eighteenth-century poets. It is certainly understandable that he was to find no response to Moréas's conventional imagery, even though one may not go so far as the composer himself in denying the attractive qualities, among the songs of this group, of the *Air champêtre*. But in the main, Poulenc's judgment may be endorsed. He had once again deviated.

The two piano *Novelettes* of the same year are altogether more authentic. The first, in C major, is a poetic piece with not a trace of affectation; the second, in B minor, is a mischievous little rhythmic essay revealing yet another aspect of Poulenc's gift for an expression in music of banter and dry wit. Another product of this year is the charming *Pastourelle*, widely known in a piano arrangement, but originally conceived for orchestra as a contribution to the children's ballet *L'Eventail de Jeanne*, commissioned by Madame René Dubost. In 1928 came the *Pastorale*, *Toccata* and *Hymne* in the form of a piano suite. The first was actually written ten years earlier as the first of three Pastorales offered to Ricardo Viñès. The brilliance of the *Toccata* has been admirably conveyed by Horowitz, while the *Hymne* contrives to mate stylistic elements of Chopin and Stravinsky. Though not of the calibre of the *Toccata*, this final movement nevertheless displays an eloquent lyrical vein. Lyrical qualities of this order are on the whole rare in Poulenc's piano music, which normally illustrates his lighter moods as, for instance, the *Humoresque* of 1935 dedicated to Gieseking.

About this time, at the salon of a well-known patroness of musicians, Princess Edmond de Polignac, Poulenc was privileged to meet the distinguished harpsichordist, Wanda Landowska. The occasion was the first performance of Manuel de Falla's *El Retablo del Maese Pedro*, in which Landowska played the harpsichord, used for the first time in the modern orchestra in this work.

Poulenc immediately responded to Landowska's suggestion that he should write a harpsichord concerto. Over the years a warm friendship grew between the two musicians. It was based in the first place on Landowska's revelation to Poulenc of a much more genuinely alive spirit in the music of Bach than he had hitherto seen, and later, during periods that the composer spent at her home at Saint-Leu-la-Forêt, of the French eighteenth-century harpsichord composers.

The *Concert Champêtre* for harpsichord is, with the earlier concerto by Falla, the most remarkable of the modern works for this instrument. In spirit the two concertos are completely different. The Spanish work is deliberately austere, almost ascetic; the French example follows those native traditions of an earlier age in which certain rustic associations were discreetly hidden behind a characteristic façade of elegance.

An allegiance to the older harpsichord composers is immediately apparent. The work is conceived as a homage to the composer's musical ancestors but not as a pastiche of their works. Poulenc's distinctive features invariably emerge in much the same way as the features of Ravel are firmly stamped on *Le Tombeau de Couperin*.

Passages of lyrical grace throw into relief the essentially voluble character of the opening movement, which is also remarkable for novel instrumental effects, notably the combination of the harpsichord with the sharp timbre of the oboe. The eighteenth century is evoked by the character of the main subject of the *Andante*, a lyrical discourse on the strings which is developed in the staid form of the Sicilienne; and with much intriguing by-play between harpsichord and orchestra the *Finale* races to a brilliant conclusion.

The rustic aspect of this *Concert Champêtre* is emphasised by the horns in the small orchestra and also by the deliberate avoidance of any kind of formal musical development. The first performance took place on May 3rd, 1929, at the Salle Pleyel, under the direction of Pierre Monteux and with Wanda Landowska at the harpsichord. A private performance had earlier been given by Landowska at her country home, in which the orchestral accompaniment was played by the composer at the piano. Jacques de Lacretelle wrote of the memorable occasion that 'the sounds of the harpsichord seemed to tinkle out a vast display of baroque art mingled with all the surprises of modern harmony'. It seemed to him to be a scene from *A Midsummer Night's Dream*.

*   *   *

In 1929, Poulenc was asked by the Vicomte and the Vicomtesse de Noailles to write a ballet for a fête at their Paris home at the Place des Etats-Unis. He suggested a choreographic concerto, an amphibious work as he called it, for a dancer, pianist and a chamber orchestra of eighteen instruments. This was the *Aubade*.

As with his other ballets, the scenario was written by the composer himself. The subject was the Chastity of Diana. At daybreak Diana, surrounded by her suite, rebels against the divine law that condemns her to eternal chastity. Her friends offer consolation in presenting her with the bow that is the symbol of her divine mission. Reluctantly she accepts it and leaps off into the forest to sublimate her amorous torments in the traditional hunt. The first performance of *Aubade* was thus given privately on June 18th, 1929. The choreography was by Nijinska and the décor by Jean-Michel Franck. The composer played the solo piano. It was later given on January 21st, 1930, at the Théâtre des Champs-Elysées, by the Russian Ballet company of Vera Nemtchinova who had danced in *Les Biches*, with choreography

by Georges Balanchine. A new scenario was provided by
Balanchine for this production, based on the story of Diana
and Actaeon. This was completely opposed to the composer's conception which was of a ballet to be danced by
women only and designed to display Diana's solitude. The
intrusion of a male dancer in the character of Actaeon under-
mined this conception.

The work, consisting of seven movements played without
a break, opens with a brisk Toccata for solo piano. The
Recitative is a sort of lyrical declamation and the Rondo
which follows concludes with an echo effect. Then come
a lively Presto movement, another Recitative in which there
is some charming writing for the oboe, a characteristic
Andante, an Allegro and the final section which establishes
an undisturbed mood of serenity. This characteristic French
work is conceived in the *style galant* of the opera ballets of
Rameau. It is a true 'divertissement', subtle in the interplay of
sentiment. The lyrical writing is wholly spontaneous.

The following year, 1930, Poulenc returned to song-
writing with the *Epitaphe*, on a poem of Malherbe. The
sober mood of this song, written in memory of the composer's friend Raymonde Linassier, was inspired by the
sight of a noble building of the period of Louis XIII. The
gap was bridged, and in 1931 he wrote the *Trois Poèmes* and
the *Quatre Poèmes*, both on texts of Apollinaire (though the
texts of the first set are ascribed to the fictitious name of
Louise Lalanne), and the *Cinq Poèmes*, on texts of Max
Jacob.

This renewed inspiration derives from the impact of the
poetry of Guillaume Apollinaire. The first song of the first

set, *Le Présent*, is required to be sung at breakneck speed with no variation in tempo; the second, *Chanson*, has the character of a children's song based on a set 'eena-meena-mina-mo' rhythm; and the third, *Hier*, explores the lyrical vein which is later so frequently associated with both Apollinaire and Eluard.

The *Quatre Poèmes* which follow immediately mark a considerable advance. Though these may not yet have quite the quality of some of the later songs such as *Bleuet* or *Les Banalités*, they clearly show the characteristic feature of Poulenc's Apollinaire songs: the borderline he so delicately establishes in music between irony (in all its degrees) and some kind of full-blooded lyricism.

Each of the four songs revives an aspect of the dated charms of the beginning of the century. *L'Anguille* is a one-in-the-bar waltz gently guying the 'corny' harmony of the period. *Carte postale* is an atmospheric interior in music in which the composer attempted to find the equivalent of Bonnard. *Avant le cinéma* is another ironic cameo bordering on lusher romantic associations; and *1904* is conceived as some sort of juggling trick with words and notes. The set was first sung by Roger Bourdin.

Max Jacob is one of the most original poets of our time. More neglected than he deserves to be, he had an influence which remains to be defined on poets as different between themselves as Jean Cocteau, Maurice Fombeure and Jacques Prévert.

There is both ingenuity and artifice in his poetry, skill and some kind of deliberate clumsiness, irresponsible high spirits and gravity, proseyness, and sheer fantasy. Sometimes it reads like a small-ad or the gossip of a concierge, but suddenly one is transported to a region where the concierge is a saint and the small-ad words of the gospel. Max Jacob was at one with these everyday folk as he was with the angels and the demons; the commonest gossip meant as much to him as the miracles of the Scriptures. His art mates a journalist's realism with some kind of other-worldly medieval mysticism. A man of the world, he retired to a monastery and ended his life as a martyr; his cynical veneer hardly hid the pure-of-heart child in him. It was this childlike soul of Jacob that produced the poetry of his native Brittany which he published under the name of Marweyn le Gaëlique. The five poems which Poulenc set in 1931 are akin to the lively spirit of these Breton poems of Jacob.

Poulenc considered these songs to be essentially descriptive, though in fact a descriptive gift is not exactly conspicuous in the poetry of Jacob. Possibly the composer had in mind the crystalline trills in the first song, *Chanson*, evoking, in the corresponding passage in the poem, the birds of the fields. Yet in setting these poems he saw clearly where he was going: descriptive they may be, in the sense that musical equivalents are discovered of the musical images.

The spirit of the poems is admirably conveyed. Of the fourth song, *Berceuse*, Poulenc wrote: 'Everything here is topsy-turvy: the father is at Mass, the mother in a cabaret, the lullaby is in waltz-rhythm'. Nor, for that matter, does the first of the set purport to be a song, as its title, *Chanson*, suggests. Poulenc immediately responded to the sophisticated note in Jacob's quaint nostalgic scenes; the last of the set,

Manuscript of *Jacques Villon*, from the song-cycle *Le Travail du peintre*

Peter Pears as the husband in the Aldeburgh production of
Les Mamelles de Tirésias

Souric et Mouric, is conceived as a sort of counting rhyme, alive and quick-moving, containing some lovely modulations and at the end a tender evocation of the sound of croaking frogs at nightfall.

The poetry of Max Jacob was also the inspiration of the secular cantata *Le Bal Masqué*, of 1932, commissioned by the Noailles. In this work, Poulenc had set his heart on some of the more extravagant poems of Jacob published in a collection under the title *Laboratoire Central*.

'I had long been fascinated by the puns of Jacob,' writes Poulenc, (le Comte d'Artois qui fait sur un toit son compte d'ardoises) and his quaint extravagance (the crippled mender of ancient motor-cars). I used the first for a bravura aria and the second for the Finale. Malvina and the blind lady (the other subjects dealt with in the vocal sections) are taken from real life. Malvina "spirals herself up as if she were dancing a gypsy waltz", simpers, sticks up her little finger to give herself the airs of a duchess, and goes to a ball in blue stockings, which is her Waterloo; conversation extends to the philosophy of Nietzsche, while all she waits for is for someone to make a pass at her: an unfortunate but very common victim of snobbery.

'The character of the blind lady was suggested by an enormous fat *rentière* who wandered round the Ile de Beauté at Nogent-sur-Marne round about 1912. She lived in some kind of Swiss-Norman cottage, spending the whole day sitting on the steps, got up in a black silk dress and making conquests. A few feet away a sort of Landru, complete with eyeglasses and vizored cap, was seated in a cane armchair reading the newspaper. When I discovered the poem of

E

Max Jacob in *Laboratoire Central*, I felt as if I were looking at an old photo in a provincial album.'[1]

The *Bal Masqué* is a musical carnival—the carnival of the Paris *banlieue* and, in this case, of one particular spot, the little outlying town of Nogent-sur-Marne. This is one of Poulenc's typically Parisian works. The untranslatable adjective that conveys its racy flavour is *Parigot*. One is taken back to the whiff of frying chips, the whistling urchins, the smart lads from town pulling a line in their drawling accents, whilst some innocent lass is being led astray to the intoxicating strains of a waltz or a Java. The music of the *Bal Masqué* belongs to the style of the early *Cocardes*, certain of the Apollinaire songs (the *Quatre Poèmes* and *Voyage à Paris*), and suggests the later comic opera *Les Mamelles de Tirésias* and the Piano Concerto.

There is an astute mind hidden in this *bon enfant* personality of Poulenc—a mind that can hold his gift for musical characterisation at a distance, refining upon it with the subtle art of the parodist, in a manner of the musical parodies in Ravel's *Histoires Naturelles* and *L'Heure Espagnole*. The whole of *Le Bal Masqué*, a secular cantata as it is aptly called, sparkles with a swift, dry wit. There are moments of lyrical charm (in *Malvina* and *La Danse aveugle*) and even of lyrical violence (the bravura aria at the opening and the Finale), but it is the sense of parody that sets this work apart. The key to the music, the composer maintains, is the Finale: 'I feel it to be a self-portrait of Max Jacob as I knew him when he lived in the Rue Gabrielle in Montmartre in 1920.' The work is written for baritone (or mezzo-soprano)

[1] *Journal de mes Mèlodiés.*

and chamber orchestra (oboe, clarinet, bassoon, cornet, violin, cello, percussion and piano). The piano is constantly brought into the foreground, almost as a solo instrument. The first performance of *Le Bal Masqué* was given at the home of the Vicomte de Noailles at Hyères, on April 20th, 1932, under the direction of Roger Désormière, sung by Gilbert Moryn and with the composer at the piano.

The Concerto for two pianos and orchestra was commissioned by the Princess Edmond de Polignac in 1932 and was rapidly written in less than three months. The first performance took place on September 5th, 1932, at the Venice International Festival. The soloists were the composer and Jacques Février and the conductor was Désiré Defauw.

Echoes of Stravinsky may be heard in the powerful rhythms of the opening Allegro; also of the Balinaisian music which the composer heard at the Colonial Exhibition of 1931. The Larghetto is based on the style of a Mozart andante, though the central section is in a rapid waltz tempo, and the finale flirts with one of those deliberately vulgar themes never far from the composer's heart. This somewhat artificial double concerto is a work that does not aim higher than pleasing diversion.

Other piano works were begun in 1932. Of the *Nocturnes* (completed in 1938) the best are the first, fourth, seventh and eighth. The fourth is a sort of dreamy Mazurka bearing a quotation from *Le Visionnaire*, by Julien Green, to whom it is dedicated: 'Not a note of the Waltzes or Schottisches was lost throughout the house, so that the sick person was able to take part in the rejoicings, dreaming on his bed of the happy years of his youth'. Chopin is evoked here, as is Schumann in the eighth of the series.

The twelve *Improvisations* (completed in 1941) contain some of Poulenc's best piano music. Influences are noticeable, and the composer was conscious of them: the twelfth is a 'Homage to Schubert', the eleventh recalls Schumann, the sixth Prokofiev and the fourth Chopin. But something original is created as the styles of these admired composers are evoked. Not over-concerned with structural problems, these are true improvisations, the first, fifth, sixth, tenth and twelfth being especially appealing. Four bars from the eighth *Improvisation* were later to be used in *Les Mamelles de Tirésias*. Finally, the three pieces (*Ariette*, *Rêve* and *Gigue*) of the *Feuillets d'Album* (1933) recall an earlier manner, the first bearing an obvious relationship to the *Adagietto* from *Les Biches*. Casting back to his early days, this last work appears to mark the end of the composer's youthful period. The charms and delights of his music are seductive still, but he is about to enter a new phase; the sophisticated Parisian world is about to be abandoned for the realms of choral and of sacred music.

* * *

The predominantly sober aspect of Poulenc's choral works is one of the most interesting features of his art. The long list, from the *Sept Chansons* to the *Stabat Mater*, includes cantatas, motets, an *a capella* Mass as well as choral works in the lighter style. The range of this body of works, both secular and religious, the majority of which are for *a capella* choir, is extensive.

The first point that requires some explanation is the surprising religious strain that soon emerges. Historical research has only recently begun to reveal the true value of the various schools of early French sacred music, and even now the purely emotional impact which much of this early music must have made is not easily revived. Also, it has been shown that the secular and the sacred styles were often curiously intermingled, and in many cases it seems likely that only the text of a work determined its classification under the one style or the other.

Clearly, no view of French musical civilisation as a whole would be valid that did not include the important contribution of sacred music. In the output of Poulenc, as it happens, the sacred works are particularly significant—a fact that has been more frequently recognised outside the composer's native country. Indeed, after the *Requiem* of Fauré, *Le Martyre de Saint Sébastien* and certain of the organ works of Messiaen, Poulenc is the one composer who has re-introduced an authentic religious note into French music. (Even the admirable religious works of Florent Schmitt and Olivier Messiaen are frequently valued for their secular appeal; Poulenc's approach to the sacred sphere is on a much more interior plane.)

Poulenc's strict religious education was continued until the death in 1917 of his father when the composer was eighteen. Thereafter, little encouragement was given to any religious tendencies. A turning-point came in 1935 on the death of his friend, the composer and critic Pierre-Octave Ferroud. The news, brought to him at Uzerche, made such a deep impression that he immediately set out on a pilgrimage to the nearby Sanctuary of Rocamadour, 'perilously situated alongside a winding road', as he has described it, 'and inspiring in those who have been privileged to visit it a feeling of unbelievable peace'. Here he was struck by 'the humble chapel cut out of the rocky mountainside, the courtyard surrounded by pink laurel trees and, inside, the wonderful Virgin carved out of black wood, the work of Saint Amadour who had climbed up a tree to see the figure of Christ'.

The evening of this visit, he began the composition of the *Litanies à la Vierge Noire*, for women's or children's voices and organ, on a text of one of the pilgrims' recitations. These rustic musical prayers, of which the organ accompaniment recalls the chapel harmonium, display the simple fervour, the mingled sweetness and humility that are to emanate from all Poulenc's religious works. The religious writer and playright, Henri Ghéon, was right in discerning in the poignant opening phrase of three notes, on the words *Ayez Pitié*, the revelation of the composer's inner soul.

In 1935, Poulenc wrote the first of his many songs on the poems of Paul Eluard, and gave the first of his memorable recitals with the singer Pierre Bernac. They had not met, as it happened, since Bernac's performance of the *Chansons Gaillardes* ten years earlier. But hearing Bernac in the songs of Fauré and Debussy in 1934 (at a private reception at the home of the sister of Edmond Rostand), Poulenc suggested their working together again on some occasion, particularly in the songs of Debussy. Two months later, in August of the same year, the first of their famous joint recitals was given, at Salzburg as it turned out, where an American patroness had invited Bernac to sing a group of Debussy songs at a midnight fête in the garden of her palatial home in Mozart's birthplace.

No one who has heard the legendary recitals of Bernac and Poulenc would question the contribution to their success of Poulenc's inimitable accompaniments. The partnership of the two artists was, moreover, exemplary in that each contrived both to merge and to throw into relief the personality of the other.

Bernac's wide repertory ranges over the German Lieder as well as the many varied styles of French song. It is an interesting fact that this distinguished French singer won wide acclaim with his authentic interpretations of Schubert and Schumann. But it is naturally in the French repertory that he excels. The secret of his art is a manner of remarkably clear and almost penetrating verbal enunciation, peculiar to himself, whereby the full poetic value of the text is thrown into relief without ever impairing the natural flow of the musical line. His interpretations of the French songs are thus unique, in that they are able to display the double poetic and musical origins of their inspiration.

Poulenc has gone so far as to declare that he learnt the art of song-writing by accompanying Bernac in the songs of Schubert, Schumann, Fauré, Debussy and Ravel. In 1935 he dedicated to Bernac the *Cinq Poèmes*, the first of the songs on the poems of Eluard, sung by Bernac at their first public recital in Paris, on April 3rd, 1935, at the École Normale. They are not more than 'gropings', the composer has stated, in his long efforts to find the musical key to the poetry of Eluard. In these songs 'the key begins to creak in the lock'. The best of the set are *Plume d'eau claire* and *Rôdeuse au front de verre*.

From the same year dates the incidental music to the play *La Reine Margot* by Roger Bourdet, in which the part of the heroine, Marguerite de Navarre, was played by Yvonne Printemps. This incidental music, based on sixteenth-century French dances and charmingly orchestrated for a small ensemble, won great popularity in its arrangement for piano under the title *Suite Française*.[1]

The following years were prolific in choral works. The *Sept Chansons* were written in 1936 and the *Mass* in 1937. Fourteen years earlier, in 1922, Poulenc had already attempted a work in the early French polyphonic style, the *Chanson à boire*, on an anonymous seventeenth-century text, written for the Students' Glee Club at Harvard. In 1936 he made a careful study of the Motets of Monteverdi, of which Nadia Boulanger had given remarkable performances at the home of the Princess de Polignac, and he now accepted a commission for a choral work from the Lyons Choir, which took the form of the *Sept Chansons*. Five of these are on poems from Paul Eluard's *La Vie Immédiate*, and two, *La*

1 An earlier score of incidental music was written in 1933 for Jean Giraudoux's play *Intermezzo*. Other incidental music was written for Jean Anouilh's *Leocadia* (1940) (of which a song in the form of a waltz is published under the title *Les Chemins de l'Amour*); *Le Voyageur sans Bagages* (1944), also by Anouilh; *Le Soldat et la Sorcière*, by Armand Salacrou; and Jean-Louis Barrault's production of Molière's *Amphytrion* (the most successful of Poulenc's incidental scores). Film scores were written for *La Belle au bois dormant*, Alexeieff's film of 1935; *La Duchesse de Langeais* (1942) and *Le Voyage en Amérique* (1951). The score of the last is for two pianos, from which the work called *L'Embarquement pour Cythère* was later arranged, a delightful piece which might be a musical counterpart of a painting by Raoul Dufy.

Blanche Neige and *Marie*, on light-hearted texts of Apollinaire. Written for mixed *a capella* choir, this work has every claim to be considered a true modern counterpart of the polyphonic works of the French Renaissance masters. Intriguing effects of contrast are achieved, the Apollinaire settings (the first and sixth) offering relief to the grave and sometimes vehement tone of the five sections inspired by Eluard. The choral writing is most ingenious, displaying original effects of solo parts made to stand out from the choral ensemble, and also a rare feeling for vocal colour and contrasts of register. Remarkable, too, are the many beautiful modulations.

The first performance of this work, for which a large choir is required, was given by the Chanteurs de Lyon on May 21st, 1937, together with works by Palestrina, Monteverdi, Jannequin, Ravel and Milhaud. The critics rightly maintained that this first major choral work of Poulenc placed his achievement on the level of Jannequin's *Bataille de Marignan*, Monteverdi's Madrigals and the beautiful choral pieces of Ravel.

The cantata entitled *Sécheresses*, for mixed choir and orchestra, on a poem by Edward James, is more ambitious in scope, though it is far from showing the stylistic perfection of the *Sept Chansons*. The poem apparently did not make quite the appeal of Eluard, though both the polyphonic and the orchestral writing have their merits, the choral treatment foreshadowing *Les Mamelles de Tirésias* and the *Stabat Mater*. After the first performance of the work by Paul Paray at the Concerts Colonne in 1938, the composer was convinced of its failure and was only prevented from destroying it by the disinterested judgment he received from his friend Georges Auric.

Whilst on holiday in 1937 with Bernac at Anost in the Morvan region, Poulenc wrote one of his major works, the *Mass in G major* for mixed *a capella* choir which he dedicated to the memory of his father.

The purity of the serene music suggests the composer's almost human conception of God. At the opposite extreme from the flamboyant examples of religious music of the nineteenth century, this beautiful *Mass*, suggesting the unadorned architecture of a Romanesque church, requires nothing but the unaccompanied choir to make its telling effects of fervour and simplicity. The *Kyrie*, the first of the five sections, is sung by women's voices only. Here a precise, energetic rhythm underlines the Latin text. The opening of the *Gloria* is sung by the basses *fortissimo* with replying phrases from the sopranos and contraltos. This section firmly establishes the major tonality. The *Sanctus* is extremely light in texture, again entrusted to women's voices, the concluding *Hosanna in excelsis* creating the impression of a vast, watery expanse. The *Benedictus* is similarly withdrawn in mood, and the concluding *Agnus Dei*, with its expressive soprano and contralto solos, reaches out to the chaste and truly disembodied ideal of the Catholic Mass.

This peaceful and most harmonious work, which has curiously made a wider appeal abroad than in its native country, was first given by the Lyons Choir on a Sunday morning in May, 1938, at the Dominican Chapel in the Faubourg St Honoré. A point of chronological interest is that this performance happened to take place on the day following that of the first performance of the ill-fated *Sécheresse*.

*　　*　　*

Years had been spent in search of a musical equivalent of the poetry of Paul Eluard. In 1937 Poulenc produced the song-cycle *Tel jour telle nuit* on nine poems of Eluard, proclaimed at its first performance as a French counterpart of the song-cycles of Schumann.

Poulenc was ideally suited to accentuate the lyrical qualities of Eluard's poetry, so vibrant in emotional warmth, so lucid in imagery. The cycle of the nine songs is here a form complete in itself: each is skilfully brought into relief by contrast with its neighbours, the fifth, *A toutes brides*, and the eighth, *Figure de force*, serving essentially as transitory songs of the cycle.

The spacious mood is set in the first song, *Bonne journée*, in the form of a poetic greeting, quiet in its assurance though scarcely hiding a hint of despair. The inspiration, the composer has stated, came from the surrealist sight of a train engine seeming to make its way through the tall trees of the outlying boulevards. An early memory was revived by this common sight in the Paris suburbs which, mysteriously, gave him the clue. The second song, *Une ruine coquille vide*, matches the deliberately unreal quality of the poem and the third, *Le front comme un drapeau perdu*, is in a lively tempo concluding, however, on an unexpectedly serious note. *Une roulotte couverte en tuiles* is an evocation, recalling some lugubrious recitative of Moussorgsky. *A toutes brides* is again a highly animated song and this leads directly to *Une herbe pauvre*, the simple fervour of which has an almost religious quality. The beautiful melody is a perfect counterpart of the poet's humble lines:

> Une herbe pauvre
> Apparut dans la neige
> C'était la santé
> Ma bouche fut émerveillée
> Du goût d'air pur qu'elle avait
> Elle était fanée
> Une herbe pauvre sauvage
> Apparut dans la neige.[1]

The seventh and eighth songs of the cycle contrast moods of delicate sensuousness and ruthless determination, and the final song, *Nous avons fait la nuit*, reaches the core of Eluard's poetry, the sublimation of terrestrial love:

> Et dans ma tête qui se met doucement d'accord
> avec la tienne avec la nuit
> Je m'émerveille de l'inconnue que tu deviens
> Une inconnue semblable à toi semblable à tout
> ce que j'aime
> Qui est toujours nouveau.[2]

[1]   The sorry patch of grass
       Uncovered by snow
       Announced restored life
       Sweet taste of clear air
       Struck wonder at my mouth
       Withered
       And wild this sorry patch of grass
       Uncovered by snow.

[2]   And in my head merged into yours and into the night
       Wonder rises at the unknown one you have become
       The unknown one like yourself, like all that I love
       Which ever must be new.

In these songs, music is somehow made to uncover unsuspected overtones and associations in poetry, and in such a way that the strength and sweetness of poet and musician are one. Eluard was the first to recognise this in the poem he inscribed to Poulenc on the occasion of the first performance of *Tel jour telle nuit:*

> Francis je ne m'écoutais pas
> Francis je te dois de m'entendre
> Sur une route toute blanche
> Dans un immense paysage
> Où la lumière se retrempe
> La nuit n'y a plus de racines
> L'ombre est derrière les miroirs
> Francis nous rêvons d'étendue
> Comme un enfant de jeux sans fin
> Dans un paysage étoilé
> Qui ne reflete que jeunesse.[1]

During the Paris World Exhibition of 1937, Harold Nicholson and other prominent English figures were entertained by François d'Harcourt. Poulenc was asked to write two Marches and an Intermezzo to accompany certain of the dishes. Other musical accompaniments were written

[1]
> I hardly listened to myself Francis
> Francis through you I now hear myself
> On the whitest of roads
> Through a vast landscape
> Soaked in light
> Night has now no roots
> Shade is behind mirrors
> Francis we dream of distance
> Like a child with an endless game
> In the starlit country
> Giving in return youth.

by Auric. Poulenc's contributions were a 'March of the period 1889' for the pineapple course, a 'Rustic Intermezzo' for the cheese, and a contemporary (1937) march at the end. Chabrier was apparently in the composer's mind for the first of these three light-hearted pieces, which might well serve as music for a miniature ballet.

Of the numerous songs written in 1938 for the recitals with Bernac, *Dans le jardin d'Anna* and *Allons plus vite*, both on poems of Apollinaire, are outstanding illustrations of Poulenc's treatment of the ironic and lyrical aspects of this poet's work. *Dans le jardin d'Anna* is a long song which has a place of its own in the vocal works. It runs through the whole gamut of irony and parody and borders on eroticism. Not only is this song a brilliant musical counterpart of Apollinaire's baroque verve: every nuance of humour and tenderness is faithfully portrayed. Period associations of Alsace and Spain are playfully dealt with in the sophisticated poem, and very artfully, a Spanish tinge is given to the opening chords of the accompaniment. Thereafter the song is carried through like some ravishing ballet in an extremely lively tempo, the piano accompaniment displaying in itself a wealth of delicious detail.

The first sketch for *Allons plus vite*, made in 1935, was discarded. This is one of Apollinaire's Parisian evocations, throwing into relief the more sordid scenes of the faubourgs where poetry was still to be extracted from the lust of loafers and prostitutes. In his *Journal de mes Mélodies*, Poulenc notes the lush Baudelairian tones of the opening lines:

Et le soir vient et les lys meurent,

Regarde ma douleur beau ciel qui me l'envoies

Une nuit de mélancolie. . . .[1]

but points out that following this noble flight, 'the poem
lands squarely on a Parisian pavement'. The juxtaposition
is accentuated in the music by a transition from A minor
to A major. The whole song is conceived in a mood of
quiet and indulgent melancholy, hardly disturbed by the
dry concluding chords.

Another Apollinaire poem long pondered over was *La
Grenouillère*. Here is a Renoir scene of full-busted women in
old-fashioned bodices picnicking at the waterside attended
by prospective lovers in striped singlets. Disdaining any
kind of timidity or irony, this song is a little masterpiece.
Even the parody of the line 'les femmes à grosses poitrines
et bêtes comme un chou' ('the full-busted women silly as
cabbages') is not underlined. The composer specifies that
the singer who approaches *La Grenouillère* must be taken in
by his own heart. The accompaniment (as in another of the
Apollinaire songs, *Hôtel*) is built on a dreamy, repeating
rhythm suggesting the lapping water around the rowing-
boats. The composer has freely admitted that it also recalls,
in a passage such as this, a device of Moussorgsky:

1   And night comes and lilies die
               Behold my grief great sky whence it comes
               A night of melancholy. . . .

* * *

From 1935 to 1938 Poulenc and Bernac were in the habit
of spending a month's holiday together each year in the
Dordogne or in the region of Morvan. Work was done on
forthcoming programmes during these holidays and new
songs were written. In August, 1938, at Anost, near Autun,
Poulenc wrote one of the finest of his songs on poems of
Eluard, *Tu vois le feu du soir*. He had seen the extraordinarily
beautiful poem in the review *Mesures* (which he bought in
the bookshop below his home in the Rue de Médicis) and
he set it to music directly he arrived at Anost. A true French
equivalent of the German *Lied*, this song, lasting no less than
four minutes, has a wonderfully pure melody maintained
from beginning to end at a high pitch of inspiration, and
brought into relief by means of a very simple accompaniment.

The last work of 1938 was, somewhat unexpectedly, the
Concerto in G minor for organ, string orchestra and timpani
commissioned by the Princess Edmond de Polignac. The
baroque associations of this work came as something of a
surprise. It is conceived in the spirit of the organ *Fantaisies*
of Buxtehude, the several movements being played without
a break. Though rhapsodical in spirit, the underlying form
was carefully worked out. It opens with an *andante* followed
by an *allegro giocoso*, leading to another slow section (*andante
moderato*) recalling the earlier Litanies. Four alternately quick
and slow sections form the remainder of the work.

The organ concerto is remarkable for the variety of its

Set by Osbert Lancaster for the Aldeburgh production (1958)
of *Les Mamelles de Tirésias*

Alice Nikitina and Serge Lifar in the Diaghilev production
(1928) of *Les Biches* at His Majesty's Theatre, London. Décor
by Marie Laurencin

inspiration and also its novel instrumental combinations. Particularly arresting is the beautiful viola solo at the end accompanied by the organ and timpani. The organ writing, which explores the instrument's various registers and couplings, is never in the least gross. The voluble character of the organ is not disdained, nor its more delicate and lyrical features.

The work was first performed by Maurice Duruflé under the conductorship of Roger Désormière and has since been widely played abroad, particularly in the United States.

—

III
(1939-1950)
The Sextet to *La Fraîcheur et le Feu*

T HE YEARS 1939 and 1940 were a period of consolidation.
Old works were revised, principally the early ballet, *Les
Biches*, which was entirely re-orchestrated. In 1932 Poulenc
had written a Sextet for piano and wind instruments, of
which he was now extremely critical and which he accordingly re-wrote. This work consists of two lively outer movements (the one recalling *Le Bal Masqué*, the other a rondo)
and, as the central panel, a charming divertimento. The form
of the first movement is somewhat incoherent, but the
admirable writing for the wind instruments is always in
character—a delight in itself.

The *Quatre Motets pour un temps de pénitence* (Four
Penitential Motets) (1938-9), for *a capella* choir, is a work of
the standing of the *Mass* with the difference that the choral
writing is less subtle and the religious message rather more
dramatically conveyed. The first of the four Motets, *Timor
et tremor*, opens boldly but soon reaches out into a spiritual
mood. The second, *Vivea mea electa*, has a long, supple phrase
at the opening and ends on a brilliant note. There is a tragic
note in the sombre *Tenebrae factae sunt*, remarkable for its
violent climaxes and its skilful use of the varied registers of

the voices, while the final Motet, *Tristis est anima*, opening, like the *Agnus Dei* of the *Mass*, with a soprano solo, contrasts moods of anxiety and resignation.

Something of the spirit of *Les Biches* is recaptured in the song-cycle *Fiançailles pour rire*. Poulenc found in the poetry of Louise de Vilmorin, the authoress of the poems of this cycle, a literary counterpart of the paintings of Marie Laurencin with whom he had been associated in *Les Biches*. Louise de Vilmorin's work has similarly a certain decorative and precious quality, the aim of which is to be irresistibly charming. Earlier, in 1937, Poulenc had set three of her poems in a manner which tastefully emphasised their attractive sentimental appeal. The six songs forming the cycle *Fiançailles pour rire* were written in 1939 at the beginning of the war, a most inappropriate work, it would appear, to have been written at this time had its composition not been prompted by a laudable motive: it was conceived as a tribute to the poet, then imprisoned in a castle in Hungary. Though the cycle was to have been a sort of feminine counterpart of *Tel jour telle nuit*, it is hardly a work on this level, nor in fact does it reflect the poet's spirit as faithfully as the earlier *Trois Poèmes*.

Of the same period is *Bleuet*, one of the most moving of the Apollinaire songs, an elegy on death matching the gravity of the poem with intense lyrical fervour, and especially remarkable for its finely-wrought piano accompaniment.

At the beginning of the war Poulenc was enlisted in an anti-aircraft unit. At the time of the Franco-German armistice he was at Bordeaux. Demobilised shortly afterwards, he spent the summer of 1940 with a friend at Brive-la-Gaillarde. There he began to sketch three new works, the incidental music for *Babar the Elephant*, the Cello Sonata and the ballet *Les Animaux modèles*. In October, back at his home at Noizay in Touraine, he began a new cycle, *Banalités*, again on poems of Apollinaire. These he came across in his library, hidden away in old literary reviews of the period of the first world war.

Banalités has deservedly become one of the most popular of the song-cycles. The first, *Hôtel*, reminiscent of *La Grenouillère*, is built around a lazy, sweet tune, a mere two pages of lyrical melody perfectly brought off. The texts of both *Hôtel* and the following song, *Voyage à Paris*, do not pretend to be anything but amusing doggerel, and Poulenc's skill and intelligence were thus put to the test in avoiding the banal settings that these particular poems might have suggested. An entirely different problem was presented by the poem *Sanglots*. This is one of the most penetrating poems of Apollinaire, exposing the misery in the hearts of all men:

> Mon pauvre coeur mon coeur brisé
> Pareil au coeur de tous les hommes
> Voici voici mes mains que la vie fit esclaves
> Est mort d'amour ou c'est tout comme
> Est mort d'amour et le voici
> Ainsi vont toutes les choses
> Arrachez donc la vôtre aussi
> Et rien ne sera libre jusqu'à la fin des temps
> Laissons tout aux morts

Et cachons nos sanglots.[1]

The setting is in every way worthy of the poem. The remarkable modulations in the piano accompaniment, which somehow reveal the inner pulsation of the poem, and the sensitive co-ordination of vocal and poetic inflections establish a unity of poetry and music reaching far beyond the idea of a simple 'setting'. Music in a song such as this has the power to fertilise words, to bring them into blossom as it were, in the way that paper Japanese flowers are made to blossom in water.

The first performance of *Banalités* was given on December 14, 1940, at the Salle Gaveau, by Pierre Bernac and the composer. The only other work of this year is the piano piece, *Mélancolie*, a rather lengthy essay lacking the composer's usual concision.

In Paris, work was continued on the ballet *Les Animaux modèles* which was completed in 1941. Poulenc had been approached years earlier for a ballet to be produced at the Opéra, and his idea was to devise a scenario from the Fables of La Fontaine. Circumstances now favoured the realisation of this project. The period setting was the beginning of the reign of Louis XIV, and the work was undertaken in the

[1]
    My poor heart my broken heart
    The same as the hearts of all men
    Here here are my hands made slaves by life
    Death from love it has just
    Died from love and here it is
    As all things happen
    Tear then your heart out too
    And nothing will be free till the end of time
    Leave all to the dead
    And stifle our sobs.

tragic days of the summer of 1940 'from an imperious desire', as the composer declared at the time, 'to rediscover in this most characteristic period of French history a reason for belief in the destiny of our country'.

The six Fables chosen as a basis for the scenario were 'The Bear and his two Friends', 'The Grasshopper and the Ant', 'The Amorous Lion', 'The Two Ages of Man', 'Death and the Woodcutter' and 'The Two Cocks'.

So as to accentuate the symbolism of these fables, the animal characters were presented as real people. The rôle of the Grasshopper is taken by a wonderful danseuse who, finding herself penniless after her hour of success, begs help from a childhood friend, now an old spinster asleep on her bags of gold.

The amorous Lion is presented as a young ne'er-do-well whose prospective father-in-law is disinclined to dismiss him without second thoughts. Death becomes a beautiful woman in court dress who only momentarily reveals her identity, thus giving significance to the woodcutter's fear.

The scene of the ballet is a farmyard on a sunny summer morning. At the opening the peasants leave for their work in the fields, and at the close they are grouped around a long table for their mid-day meal. The curtain falls as they recite the *Benedicite*, the picture suggesting a scene of Le Nain. The score of *Les Animaux modèles*, like that of *Les Biches*, is conceived in the form of a Suite. The wicked amorous Lion is portrayed by means of a Java, and the music for the episode of 'The Two Ages of Man' conjures up the spirit of Domenico Scarlatti. The contest of the two cocks inspires a brilliant divertimento. The climax of the score is the adagio illustrating the episode of 'Death and the Woodcutter'—severe, moving pages of remarkable dignity and restraint.

The first performance was given at the Paris Opéra on August 8, 1942, under the direction of Roger Désormière. The scenery, in the style of the seventeenth century, and the costumes, based on portraits of Le Nain, were undertaken by the painter Brianchon; the choreography was by Serge Lifar and the cast included Lorcia, Solange Schwarz, Yvette Chauviré, Peretti, Efimov and Lifar. The new ballet met with immediate success both from the public and the press, two critics, Auric and Honegger, noting particularly the composer's rich sense of both harmony and orchestration.

*   *   *

The war years from 1940 to 1945 were spent in Paris, with brief excursions to Brive-la-Gaillarde and Beaulieu-sur-Dordogne. Many concerts were given with Pierre Bernac, exclusively devoted to French music. In 1941 only two works were written, the *a capella* choral pieces, *Exultate Dei* and *Salve Regina*. But the following two years were more productive, and in 1942 Poulenc wrote another song-cycle, the *Chansons villageoises* for baritone and orchestra. The poems of this cycle, by Maurice Fombeure, are amusing imitations of the texts of old French folk-songs, gracefully turned and shot through with a good deal of peasant wisdom. They are not mere replicas of folk-songs, nor for that matter are Poulenc's settings: they are re-creations of a primitive peasant spirit in music, in the same way as the well-known 'Seven Songs' of Falla were this composer's own idea of Spanish folk-music.

Though folk-songs of a kind, they are true examples of the *mélodie* as opposed to the *chanson* with verses and chorus. Appropriately, the music is only loosely tied to the text. Poulenc admits having been influenced here by the particular cast of vocal phrase used by Maurice Chevalier. The cycle was first performed at a concert of 'La Pléïade' in Paris on June 28, 1943.

A week earlier, on June 21, the renowned violinist Ginette Neveu had given the first performance of Poulenc's Violin Sonata at the same series of concerts, with the composer at the piano. Dedicated to the memory of the Spanish poet Federico Garcia Lorca, this work has hardly the merits of the best of the vocal works or the music for wind instruments.

In the same year another set of three songs, entitled *Métamorphoses*, on poems by Louise de Vilmorin, were written in recollection of his friendship with the poet, and then came the well-known song *C*, on a poem by Louis Aragon, a moving little vignette like some old romance, and remarkable, too, for its accompaniment which is among the composer's most poetic pages. *Fêtes galantes*, also on a poem of Aragon, is by contrast a harshly cynical song, deliberately crude, therefore, in harmony and rhythm.

Figure Humaine, one of the most significant choral works of our time, was written in 1943. The poems of this cantata, for double *a capella* choir of male and female voices, were written by Paul Eluard during the dark years of the German occupation and are among the poet's best work. They express the silent anger of a suffering people muzzled by the invader, and they give voice, too, to an inner faith and to an underlying belief in the triumph of liberty. Appropriately, the last poem of the cantata is a great hymn to liberty in which Eluard's engaging manner becomes much more severe and earnest.

The identification of poet and musician in this work was complete. The score is an outstanding example of polyphonic writing, supple and also violent, limpid and also brilliant, leading to the great climax proclaiming the word *Liberté*. The more intimate sections of the cantata are the fourth part, *Toi ma patiente*, for the first choir alone, and the sixth, *Le Jour m'étonne et la Nuit me fait peur*, for the second choir. Here the long soprano melody, accompanied by murmurs from the other voices, recalls the beautiful song, *Une herbe pauvre*.

The seventh section, in which the contraltos of the first choir open with a fugal passage taken up by both choirs and developed to a climax at the words *La Pourriture avait du coeur*, bursts forth with tremendous fierceness. A long silence follows the close of this majestic movement, and the final Hymn to Liberty then opens quietly. Eluard's poem consists of twenty-one stanzas on the model of the first:

> Sur mes cahiers d'écolier,
> Sur mon pupitre et les arbres,
> Sur le sable, sur la neige
> J'écris ton nom.[1]

[1]
> On my school books
> On my desk and on the trees
> On the sands and on the snow
> I write your name.

The key-word *Liberté* is proclaimed only at the conclusion of the last stanza. The hymn is built up gradually and securely in a great variety of moods, the words *J'écris ton nom* being passed from one choir to the other each time in a different musical colour, as it were, until the final proclamation is shouted out by the entire choir.

In *Figure Humaine* the man and his work were one. The first performance was given shortly after the Liberation, in January, 1945, by the B.B.C. Choir under Leslie Woodgate in an English translation by Rollo Myers. It was given in France at one of the concerts of La Pléïade in 1947. It is significant that this major work of Poulenc should be not an orchestral or an instrumental work, but a purely vocal work.

Two other *a capella* works were written during the later war years: the small chamber cantata entitled *Un soir de neige* (1944) on poems of Eluard, a quiet lyrical work in four movements which can also be performed by six solo voices; and the *Huit chansons françaises* (1945) on folk-song texts. The song *Montparnasse*, on a poem written by Apollinaire in 1912, was completed in 1943, though it had been simmering in the composer's mind for four years. This is a typical Parisian evocation of Apollinaire and Poulenc, with another of those sustained lyrical lines that seem to be the product of a single spontaneous inspiration. Actually it was pieced together from various moments of inspiration. It began with a fragment written in 1941 (the setting of the line 'Un poète lyrique d'Allemagne'), followed by the end of the song written in 1943; then came the music for the line 'Donnez-moi pour toujours une chambre à la semaine';

and the following year the two first lines were set. Fragments pieced together in this way are never transposed; the composer's method is to let them settle in his mind, offering an opportunity, at the right moment, for some kind of mysterious modulation to present itself and to weld one passage to another.

In 1945 Poulenc returned to the incidental music for *Babar the Elephant*, of which he had made a sketch for the amusement of his cousin's children at Brive-la-Gaillarde in 1940.

The children's story, in one of the delightfully illustrated 'Babar' books of Jean de Brunhoff, is well known. Babar, a baby elephant whose mother has been killed by a huntsman, meets a kindly old lady who provides him with a fine suit of clothes and a grand motor-car. Babar soon begins to long for his native forests, and when his cousins Arthur and Celeste discover him he makes off with them and is elected to succeed the King of the Elephants who had eaten a poisonous mushroom. Babar marries Celeste and is last seen dreaming of his happy future in contemplation of a wonderful starlit sky.

The score is for reciter and piano. Each of the episodes is described by the spoken voice, the music being purely descriptive. Each section is a piano piece complete in itself in the form of a Lullaby, a Rêverie, a Galop, a Nocturne and so on. This is a pointed and charming score containing some of the best pages of the composer's piano music, a counterpart in Poulenc's work of Schumann's *Kinderscenen* or Debussy's *Children's Corner*.

* * *

Guillaume Apollinaire's 'surrealist drama', *Les Mamelles de Tirésias* was written in 1903 and first produced in 1917. Other composers, Satie and Auric, had been approached by the poet to write incidental music for this theatrical fantasy, precariously poised on the borderland between sheer craziness and farce. They declined on account of the inconsequential nature of the plot. Poulenc saw in it a libretto for the delectable froths of a comic opera. The French must have children is its desperate message—if message it is at all; and not all the gags of the farrago come off.

The two scenes display the hilarious confusion among the natives of Zanzibar at the sight of Thérèse and her husband who change their sex. Thérèse, an early feminist, becomes Tiresias, her breasts float up like balloons into the sky, and in the second scene the stage is crammed with cradles, the progeny of her female husband. At the end Thérèse appears as a fortune-teller predicting wealth to all bearers of children.

The very choice of this medley was a challenge: no dramatic tension and only the slenderest line of any kind of dramatic continuity. Therefore the whole weight in an opera-house had to be borne by the musical score. This grave defect becomes a virtue in this comic opera. A similar problem had earlier been tackled in *Le Bal Masqué* with brilliant musical effect, and the same results were to be obtained from the seemingly unproductive libretto of *Les Mamelles de Tirésias*.

The opera opens with a Prologue in the form of a broad, lyrical aria sung by the Manager of the troupe. This leads to the delightful Polka with its mock naivety, introducing the two comic characters Lacouf and Presto.

There follows a duet with the feigned death of these two puppets, and the people of Zanzibar, led by Thérèse, then chant a chorus conceived in the manner of an old popular song.

The entrance of the gendarme, who loses no time in courting the husband of Thérèse, dressed as a woman, brings another droll duet, whereupon the husband denounces the women of Zanzibar and proclaims the fertility of men. The first act ends in a scene of wonderful vivacity in which the chorus contrast the solemnity of a chorale with the sprightliness of a typical French rondeau.

The second act opens with the chorus gravely repeating a theme from this final scene in front of the curtain, accompanied by voices from the cradles behind. A journalist from Paris appears, quickly dispatched by Thérèse's husband who announces that a journalist is to be found among his own offspring; and indeed he, too, has an engaging little aria in which the day's happenings are one by one enumerated.

The gendarme reappears, followed by Thérèse disguised as a fortune-teller. The reconciliation of Thérèse and her husband offers the opportunity of an exquisite duet, and the work ends with a scene which is a whirlwind of excitement, beginning with an amorous waltz and developing into an irresistible gallop.

The incoherent libretto demanded that the musical value of the score should reside in brisk tempo, rhythm and general animation, and also in an abundance of purely melodic charm. The forms used are the *mélodie*, rondeau, waltz, polka, pavane and gavotte. The rival claims of humour and the heart are brilliantly accommodated. The Parisian evocations provide the lyrical pages, and other affecting sections of this kind are the chorus *Comme il perdait au Zanzibar* in the first act, all the arias of the husband, the young journalist's aria in the second act and Thérèse's aria *Qu'importe viens cueillir la fraise*. As for the raucous humour, it is essentially based on paradox: deliberately, the clownish texts of Apollinaire are provided with music of heartfelt lyricism. An outstanding example is the chorale in the first act, *Vous qui pleurez en voyant la pièce*.

The characters—Thérèse, her husband and all the super-numeraries—are of course puppets. But the composer has somehow discovered the heart in them in precisely the opposite way, it may be said, from the procedure of Ravel in *L'Heure Espagnole*. There, human characters were toyed with in the manner of a conjuror; the unreality of Apollinaire's fantasy, on the other hand, was a challenge to the musician to bring into life its underlying humanity. Allied in this way to this fantasy, the success of the score *qua* music must therefore be considered an unsuspected triumph of the mind. *Les Mamelles de Tirésias* is in fact a direct successor of the two masterpieces of French comic opera which had been illustrations of this aesthetic, Chabrier's *Le Roi malgré lui*, of which it has the same rumbustiousness, and Ravel's *L'Heure Espagnole*, of which it has the same perception and wit.

Completed in 1945, *Les Mamelles de Tirésias* was first given at the Opéra-Comique on June 3, 1947. The setting was of an imaginary town on the Riviera, and the part of Thérèse was brilliantly undertaken by a young unknown singer, Denise Duval. Although it was enthusiastically received in intellectual circles, the day-to-day public were not unnaturally scandalised, particularly as it was given as part of a double bill with *La Bohème* or *Les Pêcheurs de Perles*, instead of with works such as *L'Heure Espagnole* or *L'Education manquée* with which it is more closely associated.

*   *   *

At the Salle Gaveau, on April 27 1945, a concert entirely devoted to the composer's songs was given for the first time. The singers were Suzanne Balguérie and Pierre Bernac, and the composer accompanied. The test was severe, and the press were unanimous in acclaiming Francis Poulenc as a master of the modern French song.

Three further songs were written during the following year, *Un Poème* and *Le Pont* on texts of Apollinaire, and *Paul et Virginie* on a poem of Raymond Radiguet. The first, on a poem 'the size of a postage-stamp', is expressive of silence and emptiness; the second, a conversation piece on the water, is dedicated to Raymond Radiguet, the gifted poet who died in his very early years, with whom Poulenc had spent unforgettable hours on the banks of the Marne; and the third, a lovely miniature 'made from a little music, a great deal of feeling and from silence', is taken from Radiguet's collection of poems, *Les joues en feu*.

The three songs on poems of Federico Garcia Lorca were written in 1947. Here the authentic character of Lorca's Spanish verse was less happily matched. The tragic subject of the song called *Le Disparu*, on a poem by Robert Desnos, was a common occurrence in the dark years around 1940.

Jean Cocteau and 'Les Six'. *Left to right:* Francis Poulenc,
Germaine Tailleferre, Louis Durey, Jean Cocteau, Darius
Milhaud, Arthur Honegger. *On the wall:* Georges Auric by
Cocteau

Marie Laurencin and Guillaume Apollinaire in
La Muse inspirant le poète by Henri Rousseau (1909)

The poet's friend, André Platard, had been abruptly taken
off during the German occupation. Poulenc's setting, in a
one-in-the-bar waltz time, has the poignant actuality of a
popular song which might almost be accompanied on an
accordion. It was a direct and heartfelt tribute. The remain-
ing song of this period is *Main dominée par le coeur*, an aerial
and appropriately transparent rendering of the poem of
Eluard.

1947 is the date, too, of the *Sinfonietta*, one of the most
accomplished of the orchestral works, some of the themes
of which were taken from the discarded String Quartet.
The work was commissioned for the tenth anniversary of
the B.C.C. Third Programme. Echoes of *Les Biches* may be
heard in the chattering, ballet-like music of the second
movement, and of *Les Mamelles de Tirésias* in the long lyrical
phrases of the strings. The diminutive title *Sinfonietta*
suggests the lighter, pleasurable aspects of this score which
has an affinity with the early symphony of Bizet.

The seven songs forming the cycle *Calligrammes* were
written in July, 1948. These were conceived as a farewell to
Apollinaire, from whom Poulenc was beginning to feel that
he had extracted all the inspiration this cherished poet could
yield. Most of the earlier Apollinaire settings were taken
from the collection *Il y a*. The poems of *Calligrammes* had
been known to him much earlier during his military service
when he used to browse over them, when on leave, in the
bistros at Nogent-sur-Marne. In recollection of these early
days he dedicated each of the seven songs to one of the
friends of his youth. One is dedicated to Raymonde
Linassier and another to Jacqueline Apollinaire, whom he
G

met at Montparnasse with the poet and Pablo Picasso. The main technical interest of this cycle is in the subtlety of the piano accompaniments. In the fourth, *Il pleut*, the piano part contains a sort of musical calligram. The last, *Voyage*, is remarkable for its sensitive modulations leading, as the composer has eloquently put it, 'from feeling to silence through the experiences of melancholy and love'. It brings this last Apollinaire cycle to a close on a serious and remote note.

Then came the Cello Sonata and the four *Petites prières de Saint François d'Assise* for *a capella* male choir. Sketches for the Sonata had been made in 1940 (hence the similarity with some of the themes from the ballet *Les Animaux Modèles*) but were put aside until a work for cello was requested by Pierre Fournier to whom the Sonata is dedicated. The best movement in this work of only passable interest is the attractive Cavatina. The *Petites Prières*, on the other hand, are a splendid example of Poulenc's choral music, a true and humble counterpart of the eloquent prayers of St Francis.

In November, 1948, Poulenc and Bernac left for their first tour of the United States. Poulenc's music was now well known in America, where his choral works were more frequently performed than in his native country. Recitals of French songs were given in many of the principal cities over a period of two months and in New York, at Carnegie Hall, Poulenc played the solo piano part of the *Concert Champêtre* with Dimitri Mitropoulos.

In New York he met Wanda Landowska, Stravinsky, Horowitz and Samuel Barber. Landowska, his old friend of thirty years ago, was now seventy, and Poulenc was struck by her wonderful devotion to her work which reminded him of the similar devotion of Colette. He was enchanted by the museums, and in his Parisian manner idled along the New York streets in an attempt to take in the queer mixtures of architectural styles.

Returning to Paris in January 1949, Poulenc and Bernac began to prepare for a second American tour the following year. In the meantime a Piano Concerto had been commissioned from Poulenc for the Boston Symphony Orchestra.

The first performance of this work was given by the composer and Charles Münch at Boston in January, 1950. 'It went well', Poulenc noted in his diary. 'Five recalls, but more friendliness on the part of the audience than genuine enthusiasm. The *Rondeau à la Française*, with its deliberate impertinence, was something of a shock. I was aware while playing of the audience's dwindling interest. I had hoped that this musical picture of Paris, the Paris of La Bastille rather than of Passy, would amuse them. In fact I think they were disappointed.' It may well be that the Piano Concerto suffered from comparison with the Organ Concerto which had recently been given to inaugurate the new organ at Boston. The work was later given with Münch at New York, Washington and Philadelphia, and at Montreal with Désiré Defauw where, to the composer's surprise, the last movement was encored.

The first European performance was given, again with Münch, at the Aix-en-Provence festival in July of the same year. On this occasion the French press was distinctly reserved, arguing that the work showed no advance on his earlier manner.

It was in fact conceived as a Divertimento in the vein of *Le Bal Masqué* and *Les Mamelles de Tirésias*. The form of the work is simple to follow: two themes in the opening movement, the second movement is a typical andante and the final Rondeau, using a popular American song and also a quotation from a 'matchiche', is a tongue-in-the-cheek skit. The piano is not brought into prominence as in the traditional Romantic concertos, nor are the themes developed in the conventional manner. It is a concerto of tunes rather than themes, which is one of its main merits.

Between April and July 1951 another Eluard song-cycle was written, *La Fraîcheur et le Feu*, which must be placed in the front rank of the vocal works. Though the seven poems of this cycle were published separately, they form a single continuous poem. The component songs of the cycle must similarly be conceived as a whole: the sections are united by similarities of rhythm and tempo. The writing is extremely subtle and the inspiration wonderfully distilled. 'Unis la fraîcheur et le feu', says the poem, 'brought together in freshness and fire', which is in fact a true description of the music which illuminates it. The cycle is dedicated to Stravinsky, in homage to whom there is a quotation, in the third song, in the form of an easily recognisable version of the final cadence of Stravinsky's Piano Serenade.

(1951-1958)
The *Stabat Mater* to the Flute Sonata

THE *Stabat Mater*, written during the summer of 1950 in memory of the painter Christian Bérard, was given at the Strasbourg Festival on 13 June 1951. Scored for soprano, five-part choir and orchestra, this large-scale work is a pendant, in Poulenc's choral production, to *Figure Humaine*. Each of the twelve sections establishes a contrasting mood, the work opening quietly with the *Stabat mater dolorosa*, proceeding to an expression of tragedy in the *Cuius animam gementem*, and thereafter encircling a whole range of religious experience, from sorrow and grace to drama and majesty. Saved from any kind of baroque excess by the composer's innate taste, the writing is noticeably more ornate than in the *Mass* or the *Motets*. A long, fervent prayer, this highly individual *Stabat Mater* includes passages of musical realism (though not of mere picturesqueness), the problem having been to maintain these realistic features within an overall musical form.

Poulenc's instinctive sense of vocal writing is displayed here in a most generous manner. The two soprano arias are magnificent lyrical outbursts, and the transparent choral episodes show a consummate technique. The sober treatment of the orchestra, never merely doubling the choir, is a characteristic example of Poulenc's methods of tactful gauging. The work was warmly received throughout Europe and won the award of the Critics' Circle in New York for the best choral work of the year.

The *Thème Varié* (a series of eleven piano variations) of 1951 can hardly be ranked among the more successful piano works. The Four Christmas Motets on Latin texts were begun in this year and finished in May, 1952. These form a pendant to the *Motets pour un temps de pénitence*. The latter were dramatic; the Christmas Motets display a vein of quiet charm and serenity. The Motet for three women's voices, *Ave verum corpus*, was written in 1952 for a woman's choir in Pittsburg, and another American commission, from the pianists Arthur Gold and Robert Fizdale, was the Sonata for two pianos.

Begun at Marseilles in the autumn of 1952 and finished at Noizay in the spring of the following year, the two-piano Sonata is a thoroughly characteristic work, the piano writing being throughout most rewarding. The form is not in the least traditional. The opening *Prologue* opens and closes with a theme in very slow tempo, reminiscent of the beginning of *Les Animaux modèles*, the second theme being nothing more than a rhythmical progression. The second movement is a brilliant scherzo containing a contrasting section of great lyrical beauty. The slow movement, *andante lyrico*, has similarly pages of genuine inspiration, and the work ends with a gay piece in the form of an *Epilogue*.

Among other commissions of 1953 was a request from La Scala for a ballet on the subject of St Margaret of Cortona. The subject happened not to appeal to Poulenc in the least. An opera libretto was what he was now seeking;

whereupon the suggestion was made by Ricordi's that he might be attracted by the *Dialogues des Carmélites*, by Georges Bernanos. He read the play one morning in a café in the Piazza Navone in Rome, convinced at each scene that he had found the ideal libretto. An enthusiastic wire was sent to Valcarenghi, the director of Ricordi's. Work was begun in August 1953, the libretto having been established in no more than three hours on a train journey. The piano and vocal score was completed in September 1955, and the orchestral score by June of the following year.

*   *   *

The libretto of *Les Dialogues des Carmélites*, on the subject of the thirteen nuns of the Carmelite convent at Compiègne who were condemned to the guillotine during the French Revolution, has a curious origin. The text by Georges Bernanos derives from a short story entitled *Die Letzte am Schaffot*, by the German writer Gertrud von Le Fort. In this story the character of Blanche de la Force was a pure invention of the novelist, as indeed was the whole drama of fear in which she plays the principal part. In 1947, a French Dominican priest, Father Brückberger, and Philippe Agostini devised a film scenario from this German story, to which they added another character, the brother of Blanche, named the Chevalier de la Force. Bernanos was entrusted with writing the dialogues of the characters within the framework sketched out by Brückberger and Agostini. These film dialogues turned out to be hardly suitable for screen treatment, and were never used in the

form for which they were intended. After the death of
Bernanos in 1948, they were, however, published by his
friend and executor Albert Béguin. With the co-operation
of Marcelle Tassencourt he also produced them in the form
of a play at the Théâtre Hébertot.

In this form the *Dialogues des Carmélites* has had remarkable success on the stages of several European countries.
Indeed this adaptation of film dialogues in the form of a
play has done more to establish the reputation of Bernanos
with the wider public than any of his novels, diaries or
philosophical works. Even though the central idea derives
from the short story of Gertrud von Le Fort, the psychology
of fear which is the main theme of the *Dialogues* is treated
in a way entirely characteristic of Bernanos; and the same is
true of the interpretation offered in this play of the Communion of the Saints: 'One does not die alone; one dies for
others and even in the place of others.'

These simple words are at the core of the *Dialogues*,
and indicate too the style in which they were to be written.
The literary style of this work of Bernanos is noticeably
simpler than that of his novels and pamphlets which is often
inclined to be highly rhetorical. The beautiful lines of the
Dialogues, on the other hand, are admirably clear and direct,
no doubt owing their precision to the fact that they were
originally conceived to make an immediate impact on the
screen.

The idea of setting this text of Bernanos was fraught with
difficulties. In the first place, there would seem to be no
aesthetic reason to provide the eloquent lines of Bernanos
with music at all. Nor, certainly, do such remote subjects

as the Catholic conception of the transference of Grace and
the Communion of the Saints lend themselves to operatic
treatment. There was no central love plot nor anything
approaching human interest. These glaring defects became
the very virtues of Poulenc's conception of an opera libretto.
The self-sufficiency of the work of Bernanos incited him to
discover the music with which it should be ideally mated.

It is a commonplace in musical history to point to the
inferior libretti of many eighteenth- and nineteenth-century
operas and to revive the age-long discussions on the rival
claims in opera of the musician and the dramatist. The
perennial problem of these rival claims has not yet been
solved: there have been only individual solutions peculiar
to the few fortunate artistic marriages witnessed in recents
operatic history, chief among them those of Debussy and
Maeterlinck, Strauss and Hoffmannsthal, Berg and Büchner.
Poulenc's association with Bernanos represents a similar
marriage of kindred spirits and resembles the approach of
Debussy to the play of Maeterlinck in that the musical drama
is an inner psychological drama calculated to reveal and
throw into relief the inner conflicts of the characters rather
than features of realistic action.[1]

1 Apart from a few minor cuts, the libretto consists of the original
text of Bernanos reproduced in its entirety. Each of the three acts has
four tableaux connected by short musical interludes. The scene at the
opening is the Library of the Marquis de la Force in 1789 at the outbreak
of the Revolution. The Marquis and his son the Chevalier express their
concern for Blanche, the sensitive and idealistic daughter of the Marquis.
Blanche surprises her aged father by announcing that she intends to
enter the order of the Carmelites. The second tableau is a moving scene
between Blanche and the Prioress of the Carmelite Convent, Madame
de Croissy, in which the devoted girl proclaims that she wishes to assume
the name of 'Sister Blanche of the Agony of Christ'. The third tableau

The vocal writing is distinguished by the skilful merging of recitatives and lyrical episodes. Interest is primarily maintained in the voices, and the principal rôles are cast for recognised types of operatic voices: the Mother Superior is a contralto of the range and weight of Amneris; the second Mother Superior a soprano of a Desdemona type, and Sister Constance a light soprano who might take one of the soubrette rôles in Mozart. The orchestra, requiring triple woodwind, plays a subsidiary though discreet rôle, the

introduces the youngest of the nuns, Sister Constance de Saint-Denis, an innocent country girl who presently expresses to Blanche her fear of the forthcoming death of the Prioress. The last scene of the first act concludes with the death of the Prioress after thirty years' service in the order, a harrowing episode calculated to strike at the hearts of the assembled Sisters.

In Act 2 Blanche and Constance watch over the body of the Mother Superior and reflect that the circumstances of her death were hardly worthy of her high standing. The second tableau introduces the new Prioress and her assistant, Mother Marie of the Incarnation, who begs the nuns to pray for the dead Mother Superior. In the second tableau Blanche's brother, the Chevalier de la Force, is sent to the Convent by his father in a vain attempt to persuade Blanche to leave. In the final scene of this act the Father Confessor of the Convent announces that he has been forbidden by the Revolutionaries to perform his duties and bids them farewell. Revolutionary soldiers appear and deride the religious practices of the nuns.

The third act shows the Convent ransacked by the Revolutionaries. The Prioress begs the nuns to take the Vow of Martyrdom, to which they agree. The existence of the Convent having been threatened, Blanche is back at her father's home where the Mother Superior has come to seek her. In the third tableau, at the Prison of the Conciergerie, the nuns are huddled together in a cell awaiting judgment, but awaiting even more apprehensively the spiritual awakening of Blanche. An officer enters to proclaim that the Revolutionary Tribunal has condemned them to the guillotine. In the final tableau, the Place de la Révolution, the nuns awaiting execution prepare to meet their death. At the end Blanche arrives, free now from all underlying fear and ready to meet her fate with her Sisters. (Translator) instrumentation being frequently very ingenious. Wind instruments are prominent in the short interludes which set the mood of each tableau.

The score as a whole is conceived as a humble tribute to the work of Bernanos. The Revolution itself is no more than a remote background, totally excluded from the Carmelite convent and from the devout other-worldly souls of the Sisters. The touching musical portrait of Sister Constance, the moving scene between Blanche and the Mother Superior and the agonising scene of her death are examples of the extent to which Poulenc was able to identify himself with elusive spiritual drama. Two remarkable choral episodes are the *Ave Maria* in the second act, and the ascent of the scaffold in the last act. Particularly striking here is the double chorus of the nuns singing the *Salve Regina* in Latin and of the crowd singing with closed lips, which is so conceived that at the conclusion this double chorus forms an accompaniment to the final entry of the now emancipated Blanche chanting the *Veni Creator*. The scene before the curtain in the second act between Sister Constance and Blanche, in which the two nuns reflect on the meaning of death, has a melodic simplicity that strikes at the heart, and there is a wonderful piece of recitative in the long speech given by the Mother Superior to the nuns newly entrusted to her care. The duet of Blanche and her brother has an almost amorous lyrical quality, and there is genuine drama in the scene at the Conciergerie where Madame Lidoine exhorts the sisters to martyrdom. Throughout, Poulenc remains faithful to the traditional French axiom of the economy of means.

Two themes reappear throughout the work, the quiet, lyrical theme associated with Blanche, which is borrowed from the *Agnus Dei* of the Mass, and the agitated theme associated with the first Mother Superior, borrowed from the Organ Concerto. These are, however, not in any way used as *Leitmotive*. Formal unity is achieved through some kind of mysterious identification with Bernanos's spiritual message. 'You have both understood the mystery of the ascension of Blanche,' the Father Confessor of Bernanos declared after the performance at La Scala. 'You have both expressed the meaning of Grace.' Poulenc's *Carmelites* is in the literal sense music from the heart, a mid-twentieth-century successor of *Pelléas* and *Wozzeck*.

The Carmelites was first performed in Italian at La Scala on January 26th, 1957, and in French at the Paris Opéra on June 21st of the same year. Subsequent performances have been given at Cologne in German on July 14th, 1959, at San Francisco, in English, on September 22nd, 1957, and at Covent Garden on January 16th, 1958.

★　　★　　★

Shortly before the completion of *The Carmelites*, another song-cycle on poems of Eluard was to be written. Poulenc had long wished to set some of the poems from the collection entitled *Voir* which Eluard had dedicated to several remarkable cotemporanry painters. The plan was discussed shortly before Eluard's death; Poulenc had then wanted his friend to write a poem in praise of Matisse, to be used for the final song so that the cycle might end in a joyous, sunlit mood, but this plan came to nothing since Eluard hardly shared Poulenc's admiration for Matisse.

The cycle entitled *Travail de peintre* was completed in August, 1956, and consists of seven songs entitled *Pablo Picasso, Marc Chagall, Georges Braque, Juan Gris, Paul Klee, Juan Miro* and *Jacques Villon*. The first, depicting Picasso, is proud and aloof, the musical prosody being very spacious and the theme bearing a resemblance to the theme of Marie in *The Carmelites*. A small point to be noted is the hiatus in the vocal line before the word *renonce* (renounce) at the end, calculated to underline an imperative aspect in Picasso's work.

The second, marked *Prestissimo*, depicts the characters and animals of the canvases of Chagall in some kind of fantastic waltz. A beautiful reflective note is heard at the end on the words:

> 'Un visage aux lèvres de lune
> Qui n'a jamais dormi la nuit.'[1]

The third is a subtle tribute to Braque, offering an accurately judged contrast to the harsh violence of *Paul Klee*. *Juan Miro* opens brilliantly but leads to a lyrical section on the words: 'Les libbellules des raisins', and the final song in praise of Jacques Villon is a worthy pendant to the opening Picasso song. In this latest of the numerous Eluard song-cycles Poulenc has given of his best.

At the end of 1956 the song entitled *Souris* was dedicated

[1]   A face with moonlips
         That has never slept of nights.

to Marya Freund, the distinguished Austrian singer especially admired for her interpretation of Schoenberg's *Pierrot Lunaire*, on the occasion of her eightieth birthday. In Marya Freund's repertoire was the early Apollinaire cycle *Le Bestiaire*, and the tribute to her in this song was appropriate in that the poem was the following stanza from *Le Bestiaire*, not set in the original cycle:

'Belles journées, souris du temps
Vous rongez peu à peu ma vie.
Dieu! Je vais avoir vingt-huit ans,
Et mal vécus, a mon envie.'[1]

The latest in the long list of Poulenc's songs were also written at this time: they are *Nuage*, on a poem of Laurence de Beylié, and *Dernier Poème*, on the last lines written by Robert Desnos. The second of these has, harmonically, a resemblance to the Sonata for flute and piano written in December of the same year, and dedicated to the memory of the benevolent American patroness, Elisabeth Sprague-Coolidge. At its first performance at the Strasburg Festival on June 18th, 1957, by Jean-Pierre Rampal and the composer, the second movement was encored. The critics spoke of it as 'a great rainbow of melody' and as 'the best Poulenc and even a little better'. It is undoubtedly the best of the Sonatas, the slow movement, entitled *Cantilène*, bearing an obvious relationship to the music of Sister Constance in *The Carmelites*.

1   Wonderful days, mice of time
Which have gradually eaten into my life.
God, I shall soon be twenty-eight years old
And poorly spent as I grudge them.

V
Poulenc's Style. A Portrait

THE ART OF POULENC is in the best sense the art of a natural composer. Affinities it has, or rather had when the first works appeared, notably with Stravinsky, Satie, Moussorgsky and Chabrier, but there are few composers today presenting such an unmistakable profile. Abstract theories are unknown to him, nor has he any use for the coldly calculated mathematics of music. Instinct is his guide—a purely musical instinct and as independent as the instinct of Debussy. His individuality was at once declared in the earliest of his works, and gradually a world of his own has been marked out and described.

There have been few blind alleys, and even from these, the *Promenades* and the *Poèmes de Ronsard*, Poulenc has quickly extracted himself. *Les Biches*, the first important work, contains hardly a hint of the generous lyrical vein of the first Eluard songs and the religious works. The *Litanies* mark the opening of what seems to be the lyrical period; and in recent years several much larger works have been produced, beginning with *Les Animaux modèles* and leading to *The Carmelites*.

On the technical plane Poulenc's music is strictly diatonic, for the reason that the main feature of his art is his melodic gift. Almost everything he has written has been directly or indirectly inspired by the purely melodic associations of the human voice. Development in his music consists for the most part of a succession of melodies, and in these successions he has kept alive the beautiful and almost forgotten art of modulation. In his predominantly harmonic writing he is sensitive to the choice of key. Clarity is one of the main features of his texture, and this is especially true of his sense of the orchestra, where from work to work he has used a variety of palettes. Purely picturesque effects and doublings are hardly ever to be found.

A remarkable pianist, Poulenc composes at the keyboard. His piano works are numerous, but curiously enough the best of his piano writing is in the accompaniments to the songs. His conception of the piano is either of a percussive instrument, or of the piano which is not far removed from its ancestor the harpsichord.

Over a hundred songs form the most significant department of his work. An instinctive feeling for the human voice, together with an acute sense of musical prosody, underlie this inspired output. His choral works similarly show the composer at his best, the layout of the voices being based on an innate understanding of all that the human voice can be made to yield. One can say no more than that Poulenc writes for voices with the mastery displayed by Bartók in his writing for strings.

*   *   *

Colette has drawn a portrait of Poulenc, 'the cherished child of our age', at his country home at Noizay, near Amboise, at the time of the *Animaux modèles*. 'Fortune has

Francis Poulenc today

favoured him ever since *Les Biches*. . . . At the time of his first successes he was so young that he was believed to be affected, so brilliant that he was considered superficial, and he was looked upon as a fop. Such praises, suggesting some distinguished dignitary, were in fact addressed to a big countrified fellow, bony and jovial. I don't want to upset him; I want only to recall him in the way I best knew him. Up a chalky hill, Poulenc lives in a big airy house with vineyards all around, and there he makes his wine, and drinks it. Even his sparkling orchestration has roots in the richness of the soil. You see immediately that water is not his favourite beverage. With that strong, sensitive nose of his and the changes of expression that flash through his eyes, he is both trusting and wary, easy for his friends to get on with, a poet of the soil.'

A great-grandfather was a gardener during the First Empire at Nogent-sur-Marne. Hence, perhaps, his love of flowers and the geometrically laid out garden at Noizay, with boxwood hedges surrounding two little obelisks. Since this has been his country home over a period of thirty years, the legend has been created of Poulenc as a composer from Touraine inspired by the Loire. This is far from the truth: neither the work nor the man derives from this region.

Nor, in fact, is he the musician of the soil of Colette's portrait. The country means nothing to him; which is surely why, without distraction, he has been so productive at Noizay, turning to creative account memories of the paradise of Monte Carlo and the *bals musettes* of Nogent-sur-Marne. His Parisian haunts have been the old quarters of

H

Le Marais and the Ile Saint-Louis, the Faubourg Saint-Antoine and the coarse costermonger market of Les Halles. Regular visits were made in his youth to some of the lower music-halls and café-concerts near the Place de la République, where he gave rein to a genuine passion for the popular singers of the day, Jeanne Bloch (whose repertory included *Prostitution* and *Vierge flétrie* which he had hoped might inspire an opera) and the renowned Maurice Chevalier. These visits were often made in the company of an old schoolfriend, a champion boxer, and their girl-friends, a shoe-stitcher and a feather-dresser. A reflection of this period was the song *Toréador*, on words of Jean Cocteau.

Religious leanings have been alluded to in connection with visits to the ancient Sanctuary of Rocamadour, and the choral works from the *Mass* onwards. St Francis of Assisi and St Anthony of Padua are the saints with whom the composer of *The Carmelites* has affinities. On the score of the opera is the inscription: 'God preserve me from the drearier saintly figures of history'. The ascetic features of Catholicism are unknown to him.

Discussions of his work have shown that sources of Poulenc's musical inspiration are frequently to be sought in painting and poetry. Much of his work would indicate an abundant and easy flow of inspiration, though in fact some of his most natural music has been painfully hammered out, set aside and revised. Aware of his limitations, he has not always readily accepted commissions, among them the request from William Primrose for a Viola Concerto.

'Music should humbly seek to please' was the hedonistic motto of Debussy. Throughout the long history of French music, indeed in many of the most engaging features of French civilisation, the potent pleasure-seeking principle has been the root force; and as the seductive art of Poulenc makes its way into the heart it is clear enough that this principle is alive still in the musical soul of his country.

FRANCIS POULENC died on January 30, 1963.

CATALOGUE AND INDEX OF WORKS

SONGS   *Publisher*

1919 LE BESTIAIRE AU CORTÈGE D'ORPHÉE   Eschig
(Guillaume Apollinaire)
Le dromadaire. La chèvre du Thibet.
La sauterelle. Le dauphin. L'écrevisse.
La carpe. [p. xiii, xiv, 9]

WST - 17105 (Westminster)
S - 36370 (ANGEL)
(WITH CHAMBER ORCH)

1919 COCARDES (Jean Cocteau)   Eschig
Miel de Narbonne. Bonne d'enfant.
Enfant de troupe. [p. 10, 16]

1924-25 POÈMES DE RONSARD   Heugel
Attributs. Le tombeau. Ballet. Je n'ai
plus que les os. A son page. [p. 31]

1926 CHANSONS GAILLARDES (Anonymous   Heugel
17th-century texts)
La maîtresse volage. Chanson à boire.
Madrigal. Invocations aux Parques.
Couplets bachiques. L'offrance. La belle
jeunesse. Sérénade. [p. 32]

1927 VOCALISE (17th-century text)   Leduc

1927-28 AIRS CHANTÉS (Jean Moréas)   Rouart-
Air romantique. Air champêtre. Air   Lerolle
grave. Air vif. [p. 33]

ML 5148 (Columbia)
- WST-17146 -Westminster

93

1930   ÉPITAPHE (Malherbe) [p. 38]   *Unpublished*

1931   TROIS POÈMES DE LOUISE LALANNE   Rouart-
       Le Présent. Chanson. Hier. [p. 38]   Lerolle
       WST-17146 (Westminster)

1931   QUATRE POÈMES (Guillaume Apollin-   Rouart-
       aire)   Lerolle
       *L'anguille. Carte postale. Avant le
       cinéma. 1904.* [p. 38] Odyssey--32360009 (box)

1931   CINQ POÈMES (Max Jacob)   Rouart-
       Chanson bretonne. Le cimetière. La Lerolle
       *petite servante. Berceuse. Souric et
       Mouric.* [p. xii, 40] WST-17146 (Westminster)

1934   HUIT CHANSONS POLONAISES   Rouart-
       La couronne. Le départ. Les gars   Lerolle
       *polonais. Le dernier Mazour. L'adieu.
       Le drapeau blanc. La Vistule. Le lac.*

1935   CINQ POÈMES (Paul Eluard)   Durand
       *Peut-il se reposer. Il la prend dans ses
       bras. Plume d'eau claire. Rôdeuse au
       au front de verre. Amoureuse.* [p. 47]

1935   À SA GUITARE (Ronsard)   Durand

1937   TEL JOUR TELLE NUIT (Paul Eluard)   Durand
       Bonne journée. Une ruine coquille vide. WST-17105
       Le front comme un drapeau perdu. Une (Westminster)
       *roulotte couverte en tuile. A toutes
       brides. Une herbe pauvre. Je n'ai envie
       que de t'aimer. Figure de force brûlante et
       farouche. Nous avons fait la nuit.* [p. 51]

1937　TROIS POÈMES (Louise de Vilmorin)　　　Durand
　　　　Le garçon de Liège. Au-delà. Aux
　　　　officiers de la garde blanche. [p. 60]　WST-17146 (Westminster)

1938　DEUX POÈMES (Guillaume Apollinaire)　Rouart-
　　　　Dans le jardin d'Anna. Allons plus　Lerolle
　　　　vite. [p. 54]

1938　MIROIRS BRÛLANTS (Paul Eluard)　Odyssey 32-26 0009 (box)
　　　　Tu vois le feu du soir. Miroirs brûlants.
　　　　　　　　　　　　　　　[p. 56]

1938　LE PORTRAIT (Colette)　　　　　　　　Rouart-
　　　　　　　　　　　　　　　　　　　　　Lerolle

　　　　LA GRENOUILLÈRE (Guillaume Apolli-　Rouart-
　　　　naire) [p. 55]　　　　　　　　　　　Lerolle

　　　　PRIEZ POUR PAIX (Charles d'Orléans)　Rouart-
　　　　　　　　　　　　　　　　　　　　　Lerolle

　　　　CE DOUX PETIT VISAGE (Paul Eluard)　Rouart-
　　　　　　　　　　　　　　　　　　　　　Lerolle

　　　　BLEUET (Guillaume Apollinaire) [p. 60]　Durand

1939　FIANÇAILLES POUR RIRE (Louise de　Rouart-
　　　　Vilmorin)　　　　　　　　　　　　　Lerolle
　　　　La dame d'André. Dans l'herbe. Il vole.
　　　　Mon cadavre est doux comme un gant.
　　　　Violon. Fleurs. [p. 60]　WST-17146 (WESTMINSTER)

1940　BANALITÉS (Guillaume Apollinaire)　　Eschig
　　　　Chanson d'Orkenise. Hôtel. Fagnes de
　　　　Wallonie. Voyage à Paris. Sanglots. [p. 61]

　　　　　　　　　　WST-17105 (Westminster)
　　　　　　　　　　32 26 0009 (Odyssey X/3.1)

1942   CHANSONS   VILLAGEOISES   (Maurice   Eschig
         Fombeure)   ~~S- 36370(ANGEL~~
             Chanson du Clair Tamis. Les gars qui ~~32 26 0009(Box)~~
             vont à la fête. C'est le joli printemps. ~~Odyssey~~
             Le mendiant. Chanson de la fille frivole. ~~PAS- 900148~~
             Le retour du sergent. [p. 64]   ~~(Phillip~~

1943   MÉTAMORPHOSES (Louise de Vilmorin)   Rouart-
             Reine des mouettes. C'est ainsi que tu es. Lerolle
             Paganini. [p. 65] ~~WST- 17105 (Westminster)~~
                                  ~~MS-6151 (Columbia)~~
                                  ~~WST-17146~~

1943   DEUX POÈMES (Louis Aragon) ~~Same As~~   Rouart-
             'C'. Fêtes galantes. [p. 65] ~~Above~~ Lerolle

1943   MONTPARNASSE (Guillaume Apollin-   Eschig
         aire) [p. 67] ~~WST-17105 (Westminister) .~~

1943   HYDE PARK (Guillaume Apollinaire)   Eschig

1946   LE PONT; UN POÈME (Guillaume   Eschig
         Apollinaire) [p. 72]

1946   PAUL ET VIRGINIE (Raymond Radiguet)   Eschig
                                          [p. 72]

1947   TROIS CHANSONS DE F. GARCIA LORCA   Heugel
             L'enfant muet. Adeline à la promenade.
             Chanson de l'oranger sec. [p. 72] ~~WST-17146 (Westminster)~~

1947   . . . MAIS MOURIR (Paul Eluard)   Heugel

1947   LE DISPARU (Robert Desnos) [p. 72]   Rouart-
                                                     Lerolle

1947   MAIN DOMINÉE PAR LE COEUR (Paul   Rouart-
         Eluard) [p. 73] ~~WST-17105 (Westminister)~~Lerolle
                          ~~3226 0009 (Odyssey)(Box)~~

1948   CALLIGRAMMES (Guillaume Apollinaire)   Heugel
        L'espionne. Mutation. Vers le Sud. Il   Phil_ps-PHS-900-148
        pleut. La grâce exhilée. Aussi bien que   Odyssey 32-26 0009(box)
        les cigales. Voyage. [p. 73]

1950   LA FRAÎCHEUR ET LE FEU (Paul Eluard)   Eschig
        Rayon des yeux. . . . Le matin les   WST-17105 (WESTMINISTER)
        branches attisent. Tout disparut . . . Dans   Philips-PHS-900-148
        les ténèbres du jardin. Unis la fraîcheur
        et le feu . . . Homme au sourire tendre . . .
        La grande rivière qui va . . . [p. 76]

1954   PARISIANA (Max Jacob)   Salabert
        Joueur du bugle. Vous n'écrivez plus?

1954   ROSEMONDE (Guillaume Apollinaire)   Eschig

1956   LE TRAVAIL DU PEINTRE (Paul Eluard)   Eschig
        Pablo Picasso. Marc Chagall. Georges   PHS-900-148
        Braque. Juan Gris. Paul Klee. Juan
        Miró. Jacques Villon. [p. 85]

1956   DEUX MÉLODIES 1956   Eschig
        La souris (Guillaume Apollinaire).
        Nuage (Laurence de Beylié). [p. 86]

1956   DERNIER POÈME (Robert Desnos)   Eschig
        [p. 86]

VOCAL WORKS WITH
INSTRUMENTAL ACCOMPANIMENT

1917   RAPSODIE NÈGRE, for baritone, piano,   Chester
        string quartet and clarinet in C. [p. 7]   S-36370 (ANGEL)

1919   LE BESTIAIRE (Guillaume Apollinaire),   Eschig
        for voice, flute, clarinet, bassoon and S-36370 (ANGEL)
        string quartet. [See 'Songs']

1932   LE BAL MASQUÉ (Max Jacob), cantata   Rouart-
        for baritone (or mezzo-soprano),   Lerolle
        oboe, clarinet, bassoon, cornet, violin, S-36370(ANGEL)
        cello, percussion and piano. [p. 42]   CPT-5518
                                                (COUNTERPOINT)

1942   CHANSONS VILLAGEOISES (Maurice   Eschig
        Fombeure), for voice, flute, oboe, cor S-36370(ANGEL)
        anglais, two clarinets, two bassoons,
        two horns, dulcimer, harp, piano,
        percussion and string quartet. [p. 64]

CHORAL WORKS

1922   CHANSON À BOIRE (Anonymous 17th-   Rouart-
        century text), for a capella male choir Lerolle
        [p. 48]

1936   SEPT CHANSONS, for a capella mixed   Durand
        choir
        La blanche neige (Guillaume Apollin-
        aire). A peine défigurée (Paul Eluard).
        Par une nuit nouvelle (Paul Eluard).
        Tous les droits (Paul Eluard). Belle et
        ressemblante (Paul Eluard). Marie (Guil-
        laume Apollinaire). Luire (Paul Elu-
        ard). [p. 48]

1936   LITANIES À LA VIERGE NOIRE (Notre-   Durand
        Dame de Rocamadour), for women's   DTX-247 (PATHE)
        or children's voices and organ. [p. 46]

1936 PETITES VOIX (Madeleine Ley), five   Rouart-
      choruses for three-part *a capella*   Lerolle
      children's choir

      *La petite fille sage. Le chien perdu. En
      rentrant de l'école. Le petit garçon malade.
      Le hérisson.*

1937 MASS IN G MAJOR, for four-part *a*   Rouart-   LLST- 7/27
      capella mixed choir. [p. 50]   Lerolle   (LYRICHORD)

1937 SÉCHERESSES (Edward James), cantata   Durand
      for mixed choir and orchestra [p. 49]

1938-39 QUATRE MOTETS POUR UN TEMPS DE   Rouart- S-36121 (ANGEL)
      PÉNITENCE (Four Penitential Motets),   Lerolle LLST 7/27
      for four-part *a capella* mixed choir.   (LYRICHORD)
      [p. 59]

1941 EXULTATE DEO, for four-part *a capella* Rouart-
      mixed choir. [p. 64]   Lerolle

1941 SALVE REGINA, for four-part *a capella* Rouart-
      mixed choir. [p. 64]   Lerolle

1943 FIGURE HUMAINE (Paul Eluard), cantata   Rouart-
      for *a capella* double mixed choir.   Lerolle
      [p. 65]

1944 UN SOIR DE NEIGE (Paul Eluard), cham-   Rouart-
      ber cantata for six voices or *a capella* Lerolle
      mixed choir [p. 67]

| 1945 | CHANSONS FRANÇAISES, for *a capella* mixed choir. | Rouart-Lerolle |

> *Margoton va t'a l'iau. La belle se siet au pied de la tour. Pilons l'orge. Clic, clac, dansez sabots. C'est la petit' fill' du prince. La belle si nous étions. Ah! mon beau Laboureur. Les tisserands.* [p. 67]

1948	QUATRE PETITES PRIÈRES (St Francis), for *a capella* male choir. [p. 74]	Rouart-Lerolle
1950	STABAT MATER, for soprano, mixed choir and orchestra. [p. 77] S-3612 (ANGEL)	Rouart-Lerolle
1952	QUATRE MOTETS POUR LE TEMPS DE NOËL (Four Christmas Motets), for *a capella* mixed choir. [p. 78] LLST 7127 (LYRICHORD)	Rouart-Lerolle
1952	AVE VERUM CORPUS, motet for three female voices [p. 78]	Rouart-Lerolle

PIANO WORKS

1918	TROIS MOUVEMENTS PERPÉTUELS [p. 8] MIR 7053 (MUSIC LIBRARY)	Chester
1919	VALSE	Eschig
1920	CINQ IMPROMPTUS	Chester
1920	SUITE IN C	Chester
1924	PROMENADES (10 pieces) [p. 24]	Chester

1925   NAPOLI (*Barcarolle, Nocturne, Caprice*   Rouart-
          Italien) [p. 24]   Lerolle

1927   PASTOURELLE [p. 35]   Chester

1927-28 DEUX NOVELETTES [p. 34]   Chester

1928   TROIS PIÈCES   Heugel
          Pastorale. Toccata. Hymne. [p. 35]   Mh 5746 (Columbia)

1929   HOMMAGE À ALBERT ROUSSEL   Leduc

1929-38 HUIT NOCTURNES [p. 43]   Heugel

1932-41 DOUZE IMPROVISATIONS [p. 44]   Rouart-   LL 61 (LYRICHORD)
                                                                      Lerolle

1933   VILLAGEOISES (children's pieces)   Rouart-
                                                                      Lerolle

1933   FEUILLETS D'ALBUM   Rouart-
          Ariette. Rêve. Gigue. [p. 44]   Lerolle

1934   INTERMEZZO IN C MAJOR   Rouart-
                                                                      Lerolle

1934   INTERMEZZO IN D FLAT MAJOR   Rouart-
                                                                      Lerolle

1934   PRESTO   Chester Mh 5746 (COLUMBIA)

          BADINAGE   Chester

          HUMORESQUE   Rouart-
                                                                      Lerolle

1935   SUITE FRANÇAISE, d'après Claude Ger-   Durand
      vaise (piano version)   *ML5746(Columbia)*
      Bransle de Bourgogne. Pavane. Petite
      marche militaire. Complainte. Bransle de
      Champagne. Sicilienne. Carillon. [*See*
      under 'Chamber Orchestra']

1936   LES SOIRÉES DE NAZELLES   Durand
      Préambule. Variations. Cadence. Final.

1937   BOURRÉE D'AUVERGNE   Salabert

1940   MÉLANCOLIE [p. 62]   *ML 5746 (Columbia)* Eschig

1944   INTERMEZZO IN A FLAT MAJOR   Eschig

1951   THÈME VARIÉ [p. 78]   Eschig

Piano duet

1918   SONATA [p. 9] *SM-9023 (MACE)*   Chester
      (ARRANGED FOR 2 PIANOS)

Two pianos

      L'EMBARQUEMENT POUR CYTHÈRE [p. 48]   Eschig
1953   SONATA [p. 78]

Piano and reciter

1940-45 BABAR THE ELEPHANT (Jean de Brun-   Chester
      hoff) [p. 68]   *MIR 7053 (MUSIC LIBRARY)*
      ALSO IN A VERSION ORCHESTRATED
      BY JEAN FRANÇAIX — ANGEL — 36357

CHAMBER MUSIC

1918   SONATA FOR TWO CLARINETS [p. 9]   Chester

1922   SONATA FOR CLARINET AND BASSOON   Chester

1922   SONATA FOR HORN, TRUMPET AND TROMBONE   Chester *STRADAVERI STR-605*

1926   TRIO FOR PIANO, OBOE AND BASSOON [p. 32]   Chester *ANGEL S-36261*

1932-40   SEXTET, for piano, flute, oboe, clarinet, bassoon and horn [p. 59]   Chester *ANGEL S-36261 EVEREST-6081*

1942-43   SONATA FOR VIOLIN AND PIANO [p. 65]   Eschig

1940-48   SONATA FOR CELLO AND PIANO [p. 74]   Heugel

1947   SONATA FOR FLUTE AND PIANO [p. 86]   Chester *ANGEL S-36261*

1962   SONATA FOR CLARINET & PIANO —   NONESUCH-H-71033
1962   SONATA FOR OBOE & PIANO —   SAME AS ABOVE

CONCERTOS

1927-28   CONCERT CHAMPÊTRE, for harpsichord (or piano) and orchestra [p. 36]   Rouart-Lerolle *ANGEL-S-35993*

1929   AUBADE, choreographic concerto for piano and eighteen instruments [p. 37]   Rouart-Lerolle *NONESUCH-H-71033*

1932   CONCERTO IN D MINOR, for two pianos and orchestra [p. 43]   *ANGEL S-35993*

1938   CONCERTO IN G MINOR, for organ, orchestra and timpani [p. 56]   Rouart-Lerolle *ANGEL S-35953*

1949   CONCERTO FOR PIANO AND ORCHESTRA [p. 75]   *PERIOD-563*

WORKS FOR CHAMBER ORCHESTRA

1935   SUITE FRANÇAISE, d'après Claude Ger-   Durand
vaise for nine wind instruments, side- S-36519(ANG)
drum and harpsichord (or harp or
piano) [p. 48]

1937   TWO MARCHES AND AN INTERMEZZO   Rouart-
Marche 1889. *Intermède champêtre.*   Lerolle
Marche 1937. [p. 54]   S-36519 (ANG)

WORKS FOR LARGE ORCHESTRA

1923-40 LES BICHES (ballet suite)   S-35932 (ANGEL)   Heugel

S-36431 (ANGEL)

1942   LES ANIMAUX MODÈLES (ballet suite)   Heugel

1947   SINFONIETTA [p. 73]   S-36519(ANG)   Chester

1954   MATELOTTE PROVENÇALE (from 'La   Salabert
Guirlande de Campra'). Other pieces
in this suite are by Auric, Honegger,
Lesur, Roland-Manuel, Sauguet and
Tailleferre.

1954   BUCOLIQUE (from 'Variations sur le   Salabert
nom de Marguerite Long'). Other
pieces by Auric, Dutilleux, Françaix,
Lesur, Milhaud, Rivier and Sauguet.

BALLETS

1923   LES BICHES, one-act ballet with chorus   Heugel
(anonymous 17th-century text)
[p. 24-28]   S-35932-(ANG)

1927   PASTOURELLE (from the ballet 'L' Eventail de Jeanne'). Other pieces in
this ballet are by Auric, Delannoy,
Ferroud, Ibert, Milhaud, Roland-
Manuel, Ravel, Roussel and Schmitt
[p. 35]   Heugel

1941   LES ANIMAUX MODÈLES, one-act ballet
on a scenario of the Fables of La
Fontaine [p. 6, 62]   Eschig

Ang S 36451
(see 'suite)

OPERAS

1944   LES MAMELLES DE TIRÉSIAS, comic
opera in two acts and a prologue
(Guillaume Apolliniare) [p. xiii, 69]   Heugel

DCX-230 (Palhe)

1953-56 DIALOGUES DES CARMÉLITES, opera in
three acts (Georges Bernanos)
[p. xvii, 79]   Ricordi

3585 - (ANGEL)

1958 La Voix Humaine   *LDS - 2385 - (VICTOR)*

INCIDENTAL MUSIC

1921   *La baigneuse de Trouville. Discours du
général.* From *Les Mariés de la Tour
Eiffel* (Jean Cocteau). [p. 19-21]   *S-36519 (ANG)*

1933   INTERMEZZO (Jean Giraudoux) [p. 48]

1935   MARGOT. Written in co-operation with
Georges Auric. (Edouard Bourdet)
[p. 48]

1940   LÉOCADIA (Jean Anouilh) [p. 48]

1941   LA FILLE DU JARDINIER (Exbrayat)

J

1944   LE VOYAGEUR SANS BAGAGE (Jean
        Anouilh) [p. 48]

1944   LA NUIT DE LA SAINT-JEAN (James
        Barrie)

1945   LE SOLDAT ET LA SORCIÈRE (Armand
        Salacrou) [p. 48]
        AMPHYTRION (Molière) [p. 48]

FILM MUSIC

1935   LA BELLE AU BOIS DORMANT [p. 48]
1942   LA DUCHESSE DE LANGEAIS [p. 48]
1944   LE VOYAGEUR SANS BAGAGES [p. 48]
1951   LE VOYAGE EN AMÉRIQUE [p. 48]

LIGHT MUSIC

1918-32 TORÉADOR (Jean Cocteau) [p. 90]   Chester
1934-35 QUATRE CHANSONS POUR ENFANTS
        (Jaboune)   Chester
        *Nous voulons une petite soeur. La
        tragique histoire du petit René. Le
        petit garçon trop bien portant. Monsieur
        sans-soucis.*
1940   LES CHEMINS DE L'AMOUR   Eschig

ORCHESTRATIONS

1946   TWO POSTHUMOUS PRELUDES and the   Rouart-
        THIRD GNOSIENNE, by Erik Satie   Lerolle

DISCOGRAPHY

The following list of records has been prepared by the publishers as an appendix to M. Hell's book. New additions to the catalogues appear regularly; from time to time recordings are deleted or replaced; sometimes an old recording reappears under a new label. A list of this kind cannot hope therefore to be definitive or even wholly up to date.

We have chosen recordings from those available in America, Great Britain, France and Holland. Occasionally, we have included a recording which happens to be of special interest, despite the fact that it is known already to have been deleted. Such recordings are indicated by an asterisk.

SONGS

Le Bestiaire au Cortège d'Orphée (Apollinaire)
   Gérard Souzay and Jacqueline Bonneau
        Boîte à Musique 65 (F)*

Le Bestiaire (Apollinaire) and *Plume d'Eau* (*Cinq Poèmes*, Eluard)
   Irène Joachim with Maurice Franck conducting a chamber orchestra (*Le Bestiaire*) and Maurice Franck at the piano (*Plume d'Eau*)
        Le Chant du Monde LD-A-8079 (F)

Le Cimetière (*Cinq Poèmes*, Jacob)
   Danielle Darrieux with Wal-Berg and his orchestra
        Decca LF 1100 (GB) Special order only.

Tel jour, telle nuit (Eluard)
　　　Pierre Bernac and Francis Poulenc
H.M.V. DB 6383-4*

*Dans le Jardin d'Anna, Allons plus vite, Le Bestiaire, Le Pont,
　　　Montparnasse* (Apollinaire) ; *Cinq Poèmes, La
　　　Fraîcheur et le feu* (Eluard)
　　　Pierre Bernac and Francis Poulenc
Vega C35-A-33 (F)

La Grenouillère (Apollinaire)
　　　Gérard Souzay and Jacqueline Bonneau
Boite à Musique 63 (F)*

Fiançailles pour rire (Vilmorin), *Trois Chansons de Federico
　　　Garcia Lorca*
　　　Geneviève Touraine and Francis Poulenc
Boite à Musique LD-012 (F)

Fiançailles pour rire (Vilmorin)
　　　Gloria Davy
London 5395 (USA)

Banalités (Apollinaire) and *Chansons villageoises* (Fombeure)
　　　Pierre Bernac and Francis Poulenc
Columbia 33CX 1119 (GB)*

Banalités (Nos 2 & 4)
　　　Gladys Swarthout and G. Trovillo
H.M.V. ALP 1269 (GB)

Reine des mouettes (*Métamorphoses*, Vilmorin)
　　　Gérard Souzay and Jacqueline Bonneau
Boite à Musique 63 (F)*

Le Disparu (Desnos), *Tu vois le feu du soir* (Eluard), *Paul et
　　　Virginie* (Radiguet), *La Grenouillère* (Apollinaire),
　　　Parisiana (Jacob), *C'est ainsi que tu es* (Vilmorin),
　　　Epitaphe (Malherbe), *Chansons Gaillardes* (Anon.)
　　　Pierre Bernac and Francis Poulenc
Vega C35-A-34 (F)

VOCAL WORKS WITH INSTRUMENTAL ACCOMPANIMENT

Le Bal Masqué (Max Jacob)
>Warren Galjour and Joseph Rosanska, Daniel Guilet, Seymour Barab, Paolo Renzi, Alexander Williams, Leonard Sharrow, Harry Glantz, Harry Stitman, conducted by Edward Fendler.
>>**Esoteric ES-518 (USA)**
>>**Contrepoint MC 20004 (F)**

>Pierre Bernac and Francis Poulenc, L. Gromer, P. Etienne, M. Allard, R. Delmotte, H. Merckel, G. Marschesini, L. Luton, conducted by Louis Frémaux.
>>**Vega C35-A-35 (F)**
>>**Westminster 18422 (USA)**

CHORAL WORKS

Litanies à la Vierge noire
>J. P. Kreder Vocal Ensemble with Alain Olivier (organ)
>>**Erato EFM 42017 (F)**

Les Petites Voix (Madeleine Rey)
>Mathilde Harlay Chorale
>>**Lumen 256301 (F)***

Mass in G
>Robert Shaw Chorale
>>**H.M.V. FALP 273 (F)***

>Chanteurs de Lyons
>>**Columbia 69486-7 (USA)***
>>**Columbia RFX 61-2 (F)***

Sécheresses (Edward James)
>E. Brasseur Chorus with the Paris Conservatoire Orchestra, conducted by Georges Tzipine
>>**Columbia 33CX 1252 (GB)**
>>**Angel 35117 (USA)**
>>**Columbia 33FCX 264 (F)**

Salve Regina and *Quatre Motets pour le temps de Noël*
> Netherlands Chamber Choir conducted by Felix de Nobel
>> **Philips N 00679 R (Holland)**

Un Soir de neige (Eluard)
> J. P. Kreder Vocal Ensemble
>> **Lumen LD-1510 (F)**

Quatre petites prières (St Francis)
> Royal Male Choir 'Mastreechter Staar' conducted by Martin Koekelkonen
>> **Philips N 00617 R (Holland)**

Stabat Mater
> Jacqueline Brumaire, Alauda Choir, Colonne Symphony Orchestra, conducted by Louis Frémaux
>> **Aurora abc 301 (GB)**
>> **Vega C35-A-1 (F)**
>> **Westminster 18422 (USA)**

PIANO WORKS

Trois Mouvements perpétuels
> Grant Johannessen
>> **Nixa CLP 1181 (GB)***

> Oscar Levant
>> **Columbia CL-1134 (USA)**

Valse (1918)
> A. Haas-Hamburger
>> **Felsted RL 89006 (GB)**
>> **Period SPL 563 (USA)**

Suite in C
> Elly Kassman
>> **Griffon 1003 (F)**

Trois Pièces pour piano (1918): Pastorale, Toccata, Hyme
    Shura Cherkassky
           H.M.V. ALP 1527 (GB)

    R. Cumming
           Music Library 7053 (USA)

Humoresque in G
    A. Haas-Hamburger
           Felsted RL 89006 (GB)
           Period SPL 563 (USA)

Huit Nocturnes
    Grant Johannessen
           Nixa CLP 1181 (GB)*

Douze Improvisations
    Elly Kassman
           Lyric 61 (USA)

    J. M. Damase
           Decca FST 133527 (F)

Improvisation No. 5
    Jean Casadesus
           Columbia FCX 375 (F)

Improvisation No. 7
    J. M. Damase
           Decca EFS 450568 (F)

Les Soirées de Nazelles (1936)
    J. Ranck
           Zodiac 1002 (USA)

TWO PIANOS

L'Embarquement pour Cythère
    V. Vronsky and V. Babin
           Brunswick AXTL 1081 (GB)

Sonata for two pianos
   A. Gold and R. Fizdale
         Columbia ML-5068 (USA)

PIANO AND RECITER

Babar the Elephant (Jean de Brunhoff)
   Roger Livesey and R. Cumming
         Music Library 7053 (USA)

   Pierre Fresnay and Francis Poulenc
         Les discophiles français 425105 (F)

   Noël Coward and Francis Poulenc
         Aurora aba 253 (GB)

   Annie de Lange and Sas Bunge
         Philips S 05000 R (Holland)

CHAMBER MUSIC

Sonata for Horn, Trumpet and Trombone
   Harry Glantz, Gordon Pulis, Arthur Berv
         Stradivari STR 605 (USA)
         Concerteum CS-191 (F)

   Louis Ménardi, Lucien Thévet, G. Masson
         Decca LXT 5287 (GB & F)

Trio for Piano, Oboe and Bassoon
   Francis Poulenc, Louis Pierlot, Maurice Allard
         Vega C35-A-181 (F)

   The Koppel, Wolsing, Bloch Trio
         Métronome 3002 (F)

Sextet for Piano, Flute, Oboe, Clarinet, Bassoon and Horn
   Jean Françaix with the Radiodiffusion Wind Quintet
         Angel D 35133 (USA)
         Pathé DTX 135 (F)

Mitchell Lurie with the Fine Arts Wind Players
Capitol CTL 7066 (GB)*
Capitol P 8258 (USA)

Sonato for Violin and Piano
Louis Kaufman and Artur Balsam
Capitol CL 750*

Sonata for Flute and Piano
Jean-Pierre Rampal and Francis Poulenc
Vega C35-A-181 (F)

Sérénade (Chansons Gaillardes) arr. cello—M. Gendron
Janos Starker and Leon Pommers
Nixa PLP 708 (GB)

Maurice Gendron and Jean Françaix
Selmer-Z-8011 (F)

CONCERTOS

Concert Champêtre for Harpsichord and Orchestra
Aimée van de Wiele with the Paris Conservatoire
Orchestra conducted by Pierre Dervaux
Columbia FCX 677 (F)

Aubade (Piano and eighteen instruments)
F. Jacquinot and the Westminster Symphony Orchestra,
conducted by Anatole Fistoulari
Parlophone PMC 1019 (GB)
Odéon ODX 149 (F)
M.G.M. 3415 (USA)

Concerto in D Minor, for two Pianos and Orchestra
Arthur Whittemore and Jack Lowe with the Victor
Symphony Orchestra, conducted by Dimitri Mitro-
poulos
RCA Victor LM-1048 (U.S.A.)*

Francis Poulenc and Jacques Février with the Paris
Conservatoire Orchestra, conducted by Pierre Dervaux
Columbia FCX-677 (F)

Concerto in G Minor for Organ, Orchestra and Timpani
    E. Power Biggs with the Columbia Symphony
    Orchestra, conducted by Richard Burgin
          Columbia ML-4329 (USA)
          Philips L-01342 (F)

    Richard Ellasser with the Hamburg Philharmonic
    Orchestra, conducted by Arthur Winograd
          M.G.M. 3361 (USA)

Concerto for Piano and Orchestra
    A. Haas-Hamburger with the Pasdeloup Orchestra,
    conducted by Pierre Dervaux
          Period SPL 563 (USA)
          Felsted RL 89006 (GB)

ORCHESTRAL WORKS

Les Biches (Ballet suite)
    Paris Conservatoire Orchestra, conducted by Roger
    Désormière
          Decca LXT 2720 (GB & F)
          London LL-624 (USA)

    London Symphony Orchestra conducted by Anatole
    Fistoulari
          Parlophone PMC 1004 (GB)
          M.G.M. 3098 (USA)

OPERA

Les Mamelles de Tirésias (Apollinaire)
    Denise Duval, Jean Giraudeau, Emile Rousseau,
    Robert Jeantet, with the Chorus and Orchestra of the
    Opéra-Comique, Paris, conducted by André Cluytens
          Columbia FCX 230 (F)
          Columbia 33CX 1218 (GB)
          Angel D 35090 (USA)

Dialogues des Carmélites (Bernanos)
    Denise Duval, Denise Scharley, Jacqueline Lucazeau,
    Rita Gorr, Liliane Berton, Xavier Depraz, Paul Finel,
    Louis Rialland, with the Chorus and Orchestra of the
    Paris Opéra, conducted by Pierre Dervaux.
                H.M.V. FALP 523-525 (F)

LIGHT MUSIC

Les Chemins de l'Amour (Anouilh)
    Gladys Swarthout and G. Trovillo
                H.M.V. ALP 1269 (GB)
                RCA. A-630227 (F)

INDEX

Agostini, Philippe, 79.
Alexeieff, Alexandre, 48.
Anouilh, Jean, 48.
Ansermet, Ernest, 9.
Apollinaire, Guillaume, xiii, xv, xvi, xviii, 5, 6, 9, 10, 12, 38, 39, 49, 54, 55, 60, 61, 67, 69, 71, 72, 73, 74, 86.
Apollinaire, Jacqueline, 73.
Aragon, Louis, 6, 65.
Arrau, Claudio, 24.
Auric, Georges, 4, 10, 14, 18, 19, 20, 21, 28, 29, 32, 54, 64, 69.

Bach, J. S., xi, 22, 35.
Balakirev, 15.
Balanchine, Georges, 38.
Balguérie, Suzanne, 72.
Barber, Samuel, 74.
Barrault, Jean-Louis, 48.
Bartók, Béla, 15, 88.
Bathori, Jeanne, 5, 7, 14.
Baudelaire, 6, 54.
Beaumont, Count Etienne de, 17.
Beerbohm, Max, xx.
Beethoven, 3, 27.
Béguin, Albert, 80.
Bérard, Christian, 77.
Berg, Alban, 23, 81.
Berlioz, 3.
Bernac, Pierre, xiii, 32, 46, 47, 50, 54, 62, 64, 72, 75.
Bernanos, Georges, 79, 80, 81, 83, 84.
Berners, Lord, 15.
Bernhardt, Sarah, 1.
Bertin, Pierre, 22.
Beydts, Louis, ix.
Beylié, Laurence de, 86.
Bizet, 73.
Bloch, Jeanne, 90.
Bloy, Léon, 5.
Bonnard, Pierre, 39.
Borodin, 15.
Boschot, Adolphe, 28.

Boulanger, Nadia, 48.
Bourdet, Roger, 48.
Bourdin, Roger, 39.
Boutet de Monvel, Mlle, 2.
Bowra, C. M., xv.
Braque, Georges, 85.
Brunhoff, Jean de, 68.
Brückberger, Father, 79.
Buxtehude, 57.
Büchner, Georg, 81.

Capelle Quartet, 14.
Casella, Alfredo, 15, 24.
Chabrier, Emmanuel, ix, x, xi, 9, 54, 71, 87.
Chagall, Marc, 85.
Chalupt, René, 5.
Chauviré, Yvette, 64.
Chevalier, Maurice, ix, 65, 90.
Chopin, xi, 2, 35, 44.
Claudel, Paul, 5, 6.
Cocteau, Jean, xix, 11, 12, 13, 15, 17, 18, 19, 20, 22, 27, 39, 90.
Colette, x, 75, 88, 89.
Collet, Henri, 14, 15, 20,
Cortot, Alfred, 4.
Croiza, Claire, 30
Cui, César, 15.

Daudet, Lucien, 16.
Debussy, Claude, xii, 2, 3, 5, 7, 9, 13, 15, 17, 28, 30, 46, 47, 68, 81.
Defauw, Désiré, 43, 75.
Delgrange, Félix, 13.
Delvincourt, Claude, 24.
Desnos, Robert, 72, 86.
Désormière, Roger, 43, 57, 64.
Diaghilev, Serge de, 4, 5, 25.
Dubost, Mme René, 35.
Dufy, Raoul, 10, 17, 48.
Durey, Louis, 5, 14, 20.
Duruflé, Maurice, 57.
Duval, Denise, 71.

Efimov, 64.
Eluard, Paul, xiii, xvii, xviii, 6, 10, 31, 39, 46, 48, 51, 52, 53, 65, 66, 67, 76, 84, 87.

Falla, Manuel de, 35, 36.
Fargue, Léon-Paul, 6.
Fauconnet, Guy-Pierre, 16.
Fauré, Gabriel, xiii, 3, 5, 45, 46.
Fernandel, ix.
Ferroud, Pierre-Octave, 45.
Fizdale, Robert, 78.
Fombeure, Maurice, 39, 64.
Fournier, Pierre, 74.
France, Anatole, xi.
Franck, César, 2, 3.
Franck, Jean-Michel, 37.
Fratellini (Clowns), 16, 17.
Fresnaye, Roger de la, 11.
Freund, Marya, xvi, 23, 86.

George, André, 31.
Ghéon, Henri, 46.
Gide, André, xiv, 6.
Gieseking, Walter, 35.
Giraudoux, Jean, 48.
Gold, Arthur, 78.
Greco, El, xiv.
Green, Julien, 43.
Grieg, 2.
Gross, Valentine (see Hugo, Valentine)
Guitry, Lucien, 1.

Harcourt, Francois d', 53.
Heine, xiv.
Hoffmannsthal, Hugo von, 81.
Honegger, Arthur, 5, 14, 20, 21, 64.
Horowitz, Vladimir, 35, 74.
Hugo, Jean, 19.
Hugo, Valentine, 10, 16.

Indy, Vincent d', 15, 32.

Jacob, Max, xiii, xiv, xviii, 31, 39, 40, 41, 42.
James, Edward, 49.
Jannequin, 49.
Jourdan-Morhange, Hélène, 14.
Joyce, James, 6.

Koechlin, Charles, 21, 31.
Koubitzky, 16, 17.

Labroca, Mario, 24.
Lacretelle, Jacques de, 37.
La Fontaine, 62.
Lagut, Irène, 16, 19.
Lalanne, Louise (see Apollinaire, 38).
Laloy, Louis, 28, 29, 30.
Landowska, Wanda, 35, 36, 74.
Landru, 41.
Larbaud, Valéry, 6.
Laurencin, Marie, 10, 16, 27, 60.
Lavallière, Eve, 1.
Le Fort, Gertrud von, 79, 80.
Le Nain, 64.
Lifar, Serge, 64.
Linassier, Raymonde, 5, 30, 38, 73.
Lorca, Federico Garcia, 65, 72.
Lorcia, Suzanne, 64.
Louis XIV, 62.
Lourié, Arthur, 15.
Lovatelli, Count, 24.

Maeterlinck, Maurice, 81.
Magnard, Albéric, 21.
Mahler, Frau, 23.
Malherbe, Henry, 28.
Malipiero, G. F., 24.
Mallarmé, 6.
Manet, x.
Maré, Rolf de, 19.
Massenet, xii, 3.
Matisse, 84, 85.
Maurois, André, xvii.
Mecrovitch, Juliette, 14, 16.
Messager, André, ix, 28.
Messiaen, Olivier, 45.
Meyer, Marcelle, 4, 14, 16, 22.
Milhaud, Darius, 4, 13, 14, 15, 17, 20, 21, 22, 23, 24, 49.
Mitropoulos, Dimitri, 74.
Molière, 48.
Monnier, Adrienne, 6, 10.
Monteux, Pierre, 3, 36.
Monteverdi, 48, 49.
Morand, Paul, 15.
Moréas, Jean, 33, 34.
Moryn, Gilbert, 43.
Moussorgsky, 13, 15, 51, 55, 87.
Mozart, xi, 2, 27, 33, 43, 47, 82.

Münch, Charles, 75.
Myers, Rollo H., 67.

Nemtchinova, Vera, 27, 28, 37.
Neveu, Ginette, 65.
Nicholson, Harold, 53.
Nietzsche, 41.
Nijinska, 27.
Noailles, Viscount de, 37, 41.
Noailles, Viscountess de, 37, 41.

Palestrina, 49.
Paray, Paul, 49.
Peignot, Suzanne, 31.
Peretti, Serge, 64.
Picasso, 12, 74, 85.
Platard, André, 73.
Polignac, Princess Edmond de, 35, 43, 48, 56.
Poulenc, Emile, 1.
Poulenc, Abbé Joseph, 1.
Poulenc, Jenny, 1.
Prévert, Jacques, 39.
Primrose, William, 90.
Printemps, Yvonne, 48.
Prokofiev, Serge, xi, 44.
Proust, Marcel, 6, 25.

Racine, 32.
Radiguet, Raymond, 16, 19, 22, 72.
Rameau, 38.
Rampal, Jean-Pierre, 86.
Ravel, Maurice, 5, 8, 9, 10, 17, 18, 21, 36, 42, 47, 49, 71.
Réjane, 1.
Renard, Jules, 10.
Renoir, x, 55.
Reverdy, Pierre, 31.
Rieti, Vittorio, 24.
Rilke, Rainer Maria, xvii.
Rimsky-Korsakov, 13, 15.
Roland-Manuel, 14.
Ronsard, 31.
Rostand, Edmund, 46.
Rousseau, le Douanier, xv.
Royer, Jenny (see Poulenc, Jenny).
Rubinstein, Anton, 2.

Rubinstein, Arthur, 24.

Saint Amadour, 46.
Saint Anthony of Padua, 90.
Saint Francis of Assisi, 74, 90.
Salacrou, Armand, 48.
Satie, Erik, x, xi, 4, 5, 8, 12, 13, 14, 17, 21, 29, 69, 87.
Scarlatti, Domenico, 26, 33, 63.
Schaeffner, André, xii, 31.
Schloezer, Boris de, 27.
Schmitt, Florent, 21, 45.
Schoenberg, Arnold, xi, 15, 22, 23, 86.
Schubert, ix, xi, xii, 2, 3, 47.
Schumann, xi, 2, 3, 44, 47, 51, 68.
Schwartz, Solange, 64.
Shattuck, Roger, xv, xvi, xvii.
Shelley, xvii.
Sienkiewicz, Geneviève, 3.
Souday, Paul, 18.
Stendhal, 27, 28.
Strauss, Richard, xi, xiii, 81.
Stravinsky, Igor, xi, 3, 5, 7, 8, 9, 11, 12, 27, 35, 43, 74, 76, 87.
Sprague-Coolidge, Elizabeth, 86.

Tailleferre, Germaine, 5, 14, 20.
Tassencourt, Marcelle, 80.
Tchaikovsky, xi, xii, 27.

Valcarenghi, M., 79.
Valéry, Paul, 6.
Vaurabourg, Andrée, 16.
Verlaine, ix, 6.
Villon, Jacques, 85.
Vilmorin, Louise de, 60, 65.
Viñès, Ricardo, 3, 4, 8, 14, 22, 35.
Voltaire, xi.
Vuillermoz, Emile, 28.

Wagner, Erika, 23.
Wagner, Richard, viii, 13, 15.
Watteau, 25.
Webern, Anton, 23.
Wellesz, Egon, 24.
Woodgate, Leslie, 67.